IN TRANSIT

A NEW-FOUND FREEDOM

STEVE WALKER

Design, typesetting and publishing by UK Book Publishing

www.ukbookpublishing.com

ISBN: 978-1-916572-63-8

IN TRANSIT

A NEW-FOUND FREEDOM

CONTENTS

ACKNOWLEDGEMENTS

Thank you to my good friend, author, poet, adventurer and fellow ex-overland driver René Dee for his encouragement, help and advice in the writing of this book.

Thanks also to Hugh Barker for his editing of my initial manuscript, to Ruth Lunn for her help, advice and swift response to my many queries on the publishing process and to Jay Thompson for his formatting and excellent cover design.

A special thank you to the people of Greece and particularly the families of our adopted second home of Tolo, for their unequalled hospitality, love and friendship over the years.

Most importantly, sincere and heart-felt thanks to my dear Friend Gus Fraser who made it all happen.

PROLOGUE

FRANCE - MARCH 1970; 3.00AM

I sat behind the steering wheel of the Ford Transit Minibus – a vehicle I had never driven before, contemplating the tricky situation in which I now found myself. I was somewhere in the middle of France with a dozen passengers and my lead driver slumbering away, it was pitch dark, pouring with rain, I was on the "wrong" side of the road (I had never driven on the right - only on the left in the UK) and I had no idea where I was, or where I was supposed to be going. I was an overland driver at last!

It had all begun a year earlier. I was 23 years old, still living at home with my parents on a council estate in central Essex, working as a telephone engineer for the GPO (the General Post Office which pre-dated British Telecom), and "travel" was not part of my vocabulary, only wealthy people took holidays abroad when I was growing up in the 50s. I can remember being in awe of an uncle and aunt who had actually been to Majorca – twice!

I had left school at 16 with one GCE 'O' Level to my name (English Language), having spent the previous 5 years at grammar school being terrorised by the headmaster from hell, a sadist who took great delight in patrolling the lunch-break playground with cane in hand looking for those who were sporting non-regulation socks. As he moved round the playground the boys would move en masse in front of him, trying to keep our distance - reminiscent of sheep being herded by a sheep dog. I was caned every term for minor misdemeanours. This was, supposedly, to knock me into shape, but it had the opposite effect, turning me into something of a rebel with no enthusiasm for study.

On leaving school I managed to tie down a drawing office apprenticeship at the Ford Motor Company in Dagenham. As I was mad keen on cars and motor racing, I thought this offered me a dream career designing cars, only to discover that it was a general engineering apprenticeship designing bits to make bits for cars and very little to do with actual cars. Every third week during my time at Fords we attended the local college of further education. One week, during a Social Studies session, we were given a test to establish whether we were introverts or extroverts. I was found to be the most introverted person in a class of 18 students.

After three years of falling asleep at my drawing board I left Fords to work with my brother-in-law, Pete Ashdown who had been a Team Lotus driver before becoming the first team driver for Lola Cars and winning two consecutive British Sports Car Championships. Pete had set up a small venture making state-of-the-art lighting units for car headlamps and I used my acquired drawing office skills to design the unit and its component parts. We had just bought a second-hand Lola Mk 2 Formula Junior for me to start racing, when the rebel in me surfaced and I walked out on Pete after a silly argument. Consequently, to my eternal regret, I never got to drive the Lola.

I drifted for a while doing casual building work before getting a position in a research station, working on new compounds for insecticides. There, I became the captain of the works football team and got romantically involved with Jenny, one of the laboratory assistants who had recently married, but then separated from her violent husband. After 18 months, with a tense atmosphere building in the lab and the situation becoming increasingly awkward, I left to join the GPO, where I spent the next 18 months climbing telegraph poles and installing telephones in people's houses.

***

In mid-1969 I'd just parted from Jenny after a stormy three-year relationship and had decided that a holiday was just what I needed to get over the trauma, when I spotted an advertisement in the Sunday Express – "Young people wanted for Safari to Morocco". Geography was not my strongest subject at school – after all, why should I waste my time learning about places that I would never visit? Consequently, I had a vague idea that Morocco was somewhere in the South of France - didn't they have a Formula One Grand Prix there every year? By the time the Safari brochure arrived I'd been to the local library and discovered that Morocco was actually in North Africa. With a bit of Saturday overtime, I was earning over £40 a week (not bad money back then) and if I saved hard for the next few weeks, I could easily afford the "49 guineas" for the three-week trip to Marrakech "with a group of adventurous young people like yourself". My deposit went off in the post that day.

A couple of months later I had a bad accident and wrote my father's car off, wrapping it round a lamp post at 60mph on my way to meet Jenny, who I'd started seeing again. I was lucky to escape with a couple of broken teeth and a few stitches in the top of my head, but it changed my whole outlook on life. I had come within a hair's breadth of meeting my maker and had achieved nothing of note in my 23 years on the planet. However, having had a near death experience I now had a new resolve to do something worthwhile, something that would provide a challenge, something that would make me feel alive, so I could break out and be the person that I had always felt was there, somewhere inside of me.

1. AN AWAKENING

On the evening of the 14th September 1969, I set off on my first-ever trip abroad; although I didn't realise it at the time, it would change my life for ever. I made my way to London's Victoria Station; there, in the designated spot was a bright yellow minibus with a large roof rack complete with jerry cans and camping equipment – straight out of the brochure!

Our driver was an ex-army corporal the same age as me by the name of Gus Fraser, who had been featured in the Safari brochure. He was a charismatic figure; with his short-sleeved T-shirt, tattoos and neckerchief knotted at the side; he seemed like a character straight out of an adventure story. We didn't have people like that in Brentwood! Half an hour later, with all the passengers present and correct and our luggage stowed away on the roof rack, we were on our way to Dover to take the midnight ferry to Calais. I was beginning to live the dream; our trip was to take us to Marrakesh and back in three weeks, but it was a little disconcerting when Gus asked if any of us knew the way to Dover.

My travelling companions were a mixed bag, including two policemen from Chester, a solicitor's clerk from Wolverhampton, one New Zealander and a couple of nurses from Manchester.

I was something of an introvert and yet here I was, embarking on a 5,000-mile round trip with a bunch of complete strangers.

The ferry crossing from Dover took one and a half hours; on disembarking in Calais we set off in a southerly direction intending to drive through the night and the next day in order to cross the border into Spain and make our first overnight stop in San Sebastian. Gus was well versed in the art of breaking the ice with a new group and had invested in a couple of bottles of duty-free whisky on the crossing, which were duly bestowed upon us, the passengers, once we were under way. As the contents of the bottles disappeared, the volume of our singing increased and many an inhibition was shed. When the two bottles were "dead", more bottles of whiskey, brandy and Bacardi appeared from duty-free bags, as and when required, until a "rogue" bottle of sherry was introduced into the proceedings. At five o'clock that morning I could be seen squatting at the side of a French Autoroute with my head between my knees, feeling decidedly unwell. We stopped a little later at a village café and breakfasted on large bowls of rich, dark coffee and freshly-baked croissants while Gus went across the road to a little patisserie and came back with a box full of exquisite strawberry tarts. Breakfast would never be quite the same again. As we travelled down through France I drank in the unfamiliar scenery, towns, villages and chateaux. It was all a new, stimulating experience.

We arrived in San Sebastian at 7.00pm that evening and camped in the hills above the town at Camping Rosselada. My culinary introduction to Spain consisted of tortilla and chips, washed down with "San Miguel" Rioja. It tasted wonderful. I retired later to spend my first night under canvas and slept like a baby. We were dragged from our slumbers early the next morning by

Gus who, as we were to discover during the trip, took a perverse delight in rousing his passengers at the break of dawn. I think it must have had something to do with his army training.

After a quick breakfast we were heading through the Basque mountains towards Burgos and then on across the high plains to Madrid, a stunning city of fine buildings, wide avenues and fountains. We camped at Aranquez, about 50km south of the city. It was a beautiful campsite with tall poplar trees growing beside a meandering river; the warm night air was filled with the song of nightingales. After another early start we continued south through the wine growing region of Valdepñeas before climbing up into the Sierra Nevada toward Granada and the splendour of the Alhambra Palace.

We continued over the Sierra Nevada before dropping down to the Costa del Sol and the startling blue of the Mediterranean. I had never seen a sea quite like this, other than on a postcard. Having only experienced the North Sea and the English Channel on holidays as a child, didn't think that any sea could be that stunning shade of blue in reality. We drove along the coast road and camped that night at San Roque in the hills above Gibraltar, a beautiful place surrounded by bougainvillea and bathed in the heady scent of jasmine that carried on the evening breeze to assault the senses.

***

It was here that we met up with another group from "Safari"; that evening we discovered Anise together. It is a Spanish beverage that the barman informed us had sent many a Spaniard either blind or towards an early grave. He refused to take our money for the drinks and watched with disdain as we slowly disintegrated under the influence of the evil brew. After decanting ourselves from the bar in the early hours we staggered back to our igloo tents to continue with our drunken revelries accompanied by the instigator of the evening's festivities, Frank McGrath. He was a tall, bearded Irishman with an air of mischief about him who was the driver from the other group. Eventually, one by one we collapsed into our sleeping bags.

Our igloo tents were basically a large canvas bag with an integral ground sheet, held upright by 4 inflatable ribs that met at the top of the tent where the valve was positioned. Frank thought it would be great fun, once we were all tucked up for the night, to collapse our igloos by undoing the valves and amid a lot of angry and confused shouting (and I have to say, some very ripe language) Frank was confronted by our very angry Kiwi brandishing a large Bowie knife. The ensuing fracas was broken up by one of our Chester coppers, Mick the Plod (as he had been christened by the group), who had "retired" earlier to his tent with one of the nurses. He appeared from his rapidly collapsing igloo dressed in nothing but his Y-fronts, trying to do his British bobby bit, albeit not with much conviction: – "OK lads, let's calm it down". Frank would pay dearly for his skulduggery a few days later.

We awoke bleary-eyed at an indecently early hour thanks to our driver's enthusiasm for early starts. Back then the border between Spain and Gibraltar was sealed off by the Spanish, so we drove just along the coast to Algeciras where we boarded the ferry that took us across the Straits of Gibraltar, arriving in Ceuta an hour and a half later. Ceuta is a Spanish enclave and duty-free port on the northern tip of Morocco where we stocked up with Bacardi and Johnny Walker at 55 pesetas (about 35 pence) for a litre bottle. After a short stop of about half an hour we crossed the border into Morocco and made the short journey to Tangier, a dazzlingly white city with sun-bleached boulevards thronging with veiled women and men in their flowing djellabas.

The campsite was dry and dusty with a few palm trees providing scant relief from the full heat of the sun. I was on the western outskirts of the city, it was reached by negotiating an area known in overland circles as "Suicide Alley", as you had to be extremely careful not to "collect" several of the local residents as you drove through.

The following morning, we joined the bustle of the kasbah. The air was rich with the smell of exotic herbs and spices and the stalls full of strange fruits and sweetmeats. We were plied with glasses of sweet mint tea as traders tried to coax us into buying their rugs, brass ware and brightly-coloured kaftans at their "best price". That evening we were introduced to the delights of Moroccan cuisine, dining on couscous at a local restaurant while being entertained by Moulay, who danced with a large brass tray containing glasses of mint tea and candles, balanced on his head. As the evening progressed the tempo of the music increased and we found ourselves entranced by the grace of a belly dancer who swayed seductively to the rhythmic beat of the haunting music.

We took our revenge on Frank McGrath the following evening. A barbeque, complete with Moroccan musicians and dancers had been organized for our groups on the outskirts of the city.

Gus happened to have some kippers that had been given to him as a "thank you" by his previous group about two weeks earlier. They had been sitting in the back of the minibus ripening rather rapidly in the heat on the journey down through Spain and acquiring a very distinctive eye-watering and nose-wrinkling aroma. Once the evenings proceedings were under way and had everyone's full attention, Gus, Mick the Plod and I sneaked away and made our way over to Frank's unattended bus. We lifted the bonnet and placed a kipper on top of the engine, which could be easily found. The next was tied to the exhaust manifold – a bit more difficult to locate, and the third attached to the exhaust tail pipe. The final fish was cut into small pieces and inserted into the fresh air vents along the top of the dashboard. Job done we rejoined the festivities before our absence had been noted.

***

We broke camp the next morning and drove over the Rif Mountains where, in 1921, Abd el-Krim and his Riffian army defeated a Spanish army of 60,000 men. In three weeks of fierce battles, 18,000 Spanish troops were killed. We were scheduled to stop in Meknes to take in the Roman ruins, but Gus persuaded us to make the short drive through to Fez and its souk, a stunning kaleidoscope of brightly coloured hanks of wool drying in the sun, with air that was heavy with the smell of leather from the tanneries. Having made up a day by not staying in Meknes, Gus suggested that, rather than following our set itinerary, it might be more interesting; to go "off piste". With the consent of his gullible passengers, we travelled east towards the Algerian border and then south through the desert on a dirt road. Stopping in a small town late that afternoon we bought some chickens for our evening meal; not the slimy, white supermarket variety wrapped in plastic, but the strutting, clucking, feathered variety, which were swiftly dispatched and rendered kitchen-worthy by Gus using his army-acquired culinary skills. Later we learnt that that we had been very lucky not to hit a landmine, as the border area through which we had just travelled was politically sensitive and was rumoured to be quite heavily mined. We really had been off the beaten track. That evening we made camp in a dried river bed and feasted on barbequed chicken, before going to sleep under the stars.

The next morning, we headed west, following a rough track for a few hours; eventually it linked up with a road that took us to our next scheduled stop at Meski. To this day I don't know if it was just luck or good judgement that bought us out on the right road. Meski was an oasis on the edge of the Sahara where the French Foreign Legion had, in years gone by, constructed a swimming pool for their officers. It was fed by cool mountain springs running down from the High Atlas and surrounded by date palms. Frank McGrath had arrived with his group the previous day, who were relaxing around the pool. As we drove down into the oasis Frank saw us coming and made a frantic dash for his Transit in order to lock the doors; in his haste to get there he stumbled straight into a very smelly bog. It transpired that within ten minutes of leaving Tangier, it had become evident to Frank and his group that the bus had been "spiked" with something rather smelly and unpleasant. They soon discovered the kipper on top of the engine and set off once more, only to stop a little later with the smell of baked kipper still assaulting their nostrils. The second and third fish were eventually located and disposed of, but unfortunately the over-ripened pieces in the air vents had not been found and a somewhat "rancid" odour had accompanied their journey for the next two days until they reached Marrakesh, even with all the windows wide open. Frank had correctly deduced that the "Fraser" group had been instrumental in the sabotaging of his bus which explained his panicked dash on our arrival. We spent the next day at Meski swimming and generally relaxing after our trek across the desert, while for one dirham the lads from the local village would shin up the palm trees and gather dates for us.

The next leg of our journey took us up into the High Atlas Mountains, where Berber children stood at the road side in the chill mountain air selling rock crystals and pieces of desert rose, before we dropped down into the heat and bustle of Marrakesh where the "blue men", Tuareg nomads from the Sahara in their indigo blue robes, came to trade their camels. We stayed at the Mahmoud Hotel at the edge of the Jemaa-el-Fnaa square in front of the souk – the throbbing heart of the city. Every day, late in the afternoon, the square metamorphosed from a food market with its fruit juice traders, water sellers and snack stalls into street theatre with an exotic mixture of storytellers, musicians, healers, magicians, peddlers, jugglers, dancers, snake charmers and traditional medicine sellers. The heady mix of colours, scents, sights and the ceaseless beat of drums made it an intoxicating and unforgettable experience.

The souks of Marrakesh began on the northern edge of Jemaa-el-Fnaa, spreading through a maze of passageways and streets. They were divided into various professions selling traditional clothes, fabrics, food, spices, pottery, jewellery and many other traditional Moroccan products. The merchants insisted on plying us with the traditional mint tea before the customary bartering for goods began. Some of the more unscrupulous members of their fraternity made a habit of "spiking" the tea with kif, a local form of hashish, with the intention of making their customers more amenable when the bartering began. This tended to have the desired effect and some very odd souvenirs (including dried donkey's testicles, would you believe), were purchased at vastly inflated prices!

Every morning we ran the gauntlet of small children selling strings of brightly coloured beads outside the hotel. These beads, wound around the wrist, would become the trademark of the overland driver over the next few years. As we made our way down the road the children would crowd around us, tugging good naturedly at our sleeves, imploring us with admirable dramatics to buy their beads and hugely enjoying the whole business. These children were quite remarkable, as many of them were able to speak not only their second language of French, but also to converse quite competently in English, German, Spanish, Italian and even Dutch – and most of them were no older than ten years old.

We left Marrakesh after three magical days and returned to Tangier along the coast road via Casablanca, a disappointing city of modern buildings and no Humphrey Bogart. From Tangier we retraced our route through Spain and France to arrive back at Victoria Station, travel weary, but with a sense of fulfillment and satisfaction after our three-week adventure.

***

In 1969 "flower power" was the order of the day and we had travelled to Morocco and back to the strains of "Marrakesh Express" by Crosby, Stills and Nash which was high in the UK music charts at that time. I returned to England a changed person, finding it impossible to settle back into a daily routine and my work as a telephone engineer, as it slowly dawned on me that there was more to life than working nine to five, five days a week with three weeks holiday each year. There were exciting places to visit, wonderful sights to be seen, friends made and adventure to be found - something that was in short supply in central Essex in the late sixties. I grew a beard on that trip and looking back, although I was by then in my early twenties, it probably signalled my final step from adolescence to manhood.

The group organised a reunion in Manchester at the end of October, attended by Gus – by all accounts it was the only group reunion that he ever attended. Having downed the odd pint or two of the local" brew" and feeling happily mellow, I casually asked Gus if he wanted a co-driver the following year. He told me that he was moving from Safari to a new company, Frontier International, and they weren't employing co-drivers – but he'd get me a job as a driver if I was interested. I took this with a large pinch of salt and casually agreed, being pretty sure that nothing would come of this offer and I would never hear from the intrepid Mr Fraser again.

1969 Safari brochure

Frank McGrath
– Safari brochure photo

Gus Fraser
– Safari brochure photo

2. AN OVERLAND INDUCTION

The following January, as I returned from work at 5pm, the 'phone rang; it was Gus. He was in a pub in Earls Court Road with Colin Payten who, with his younger brother Barry, had set up Frontier International some 18 months earlier. He said that, if I could get up there, he would fix me up with a job as a driver. I started to panic. How was I going to respond when Mr Payten started asking questions, after all I had only been abroad the once – as a passenger on Gus's Morocco trip with Safari. Gus told me not to worry; he'd told Colin that I'd been his co-driver with Safari for the previous couple of years. Gus would do all the talking; all I had to do was go along with whatever he said.

I changed into my one and only suit, a natty little green number from Burtons, and jumped on a train to London. An hour or so later I found Gus and my prospective employer sitting in a corner of the King's Head. Gus introduced me to Colin, got me a drink and started talking about the various trips on which I had supposedly accompanied him over the last two years. Now I have to point out that Gus was in the premier league when it came to bull-shitting. It transpired that I had travelled extensively across Europe and North Africa and was well acquainted with both Ford Transits and Land Rovers. Furthermore, I was apparently a very capable co-driver and was ready to be given my own minibus and become a fully-fledged overland driver. I was quite impressed and began to warm to my new-found identity! I sat there in the corner and gave the occasional nod and grunt in what I considered to be the appropriate places, as Gus expounded on our exploits together.

At closing time Colin looked me square in the eye, hesitated for a split second, and then announced that there was a job for me if I wanted it. He was impressed with my track record, remarking on the fact that I had obviously been around a bit and knew the ropes and was ready to take on the job as a driver! He would be in touch to give me details of my first trip - probably in a couple of months' time. I sat on the train back to Brentwood and wondered for the first time what the hell I had just got myself into.

The following day, when I announced that I would be leaving my employ with the GPO to take up my new career as an overland driver, I was given a strong lecture by my father. He considered me mentally deranged to even be thinking about giving up a secure future and a "job for life" for the insecurity of life on the road. In 1942 my father had been taken away from a budding career as an accountant with a large oil company in London to engage in the fight against the Japanese in Burma, leaving behind his wife and two young children. When he had returned in the spring of 1945 there was no job waiting for him, and his children – my brother aged 5 and sister 7, had been strangers to him. I arrived approximately nine months later. He found work as a wages clerk at the local council offices and worked in the evenings as an operator at the local telephone exchange in order to supplement his meagre council wages and give his family a reasonable standard of living. Dad was, understandably, very focused on a secure lifestyle having had a rosy future snatched away from him in his prime; consequently, we had been given a somewhat sheltered upbringing.

At the tender age of 24 I had lived at home all my life, in the same town. I had my meals cooked for me, my washing done and my bed made for me. My travels had consisted, apart from family holidays to Walton-on-the-Naze and the Isle of Wight, of going to various car race meetings around the country from the age of 10 with my brother-in-law Pete Ashdown, one of the top racing drivers in the country in the late 50s and early 60s. When I left Grammar School at the age of 16 all I wanted to do was drive racing cars, but back then it was beyond the reach of someone bought up on an Essex council estate. Pete gave me my first driving lesson around Silverstone when I was 15 and I had many of his good driving skills instilled into me as a lad while travelling to race meetings with him.

"Overland" was a rapidly growing part of the travel industry by the late 60s, offering affordable adventure holidays for young people. It provided them with the security of travelling in a group to countries and places that might otherwise, at that time, have presented a risk for someone travelling alone. The late 60s and early 70s was an amazing period of Woodstock, peace, love and flower power – and there was a feeling of freedom in the air. The fruits of the post-war baby boom were discovering and celebrating this new-found freedom and the time was ripe for this travel phenomenon to take off.

Overland was about to provide me with an outlet for the frustrated racing driver inside of me and, until now, my unrealised search for adventure.

3. THE FIRST TRIP

t the end of January, I was invited to attend a "Frontier" reunion party in Crawley, where the guests included many of the passengers from the previous year and drivers, both old and new. I was back with Jenny again by this time and invited her to join me. For the first time in the three and a half years I had known her, she seemed out of her depth. Gone was the confident, smiling Jenny, replaced by a quiet, nervous and unassured young lady – a shadow of her former self. In retrospect, I think maybe she realised that I was moving on and she was losing me. I never saw or heard from Jenny again after that weekend.

We spent most of the evening chatting with Gus and being introduced to the other drivers, several of whom had made the transfer from Safari to Frontier along with Gus. These included a character by the name of Micky Hines

who spent the evening remarking on how strange it was that we had not met on the road the previous year. Micky had left his home town in Ireland to join a road building gang in the Australian outback, before coming to England to work as a psychiatric nurse. I'm not sure how, but somehow or other he'd ended up working for Safari, although he wasn't your typical overland driver as featured in the brochure, being short and stocky, balding and, on first impressions, rather dour. He had, apparently, met up with Gus on several occasions and could not remember having seen me with him. I muttered something to the effect that I didn't remember seeing him either (which was actually true!), but that I did tend to keep a low profile.

Colin Payten rang me in March to tell me that I would be leaving at the end of the month on a trip to Morocco. I handed in my notice to the GPO and a week later moved down to Brighton, where Gus was based. He had a good friend called Hans Happe, a German trainee manager for a large pharmaceutical company, who shared a flat at 5 Granville Road in Hove with Andy who was half Welsh and half Canadian, and Dimitris, a Greek whose father owned a large leather tannery in Istanbul and was at college studying the latest techniques in leather production. Gus wasn't exactly sofa-surfing, but he dossed down on their sofa during the "dormant" winter months and in between summer trips. On my arrival in Brighton, he introduced me to the three lads and off we went to spend the evening in the Temple Bar, their local pub.

At chucking-out time we wandered back to the flat and it seemed to go without saying that I would unroll my sleeping bag and avail myself of the lounge floor – Gus naturally commandeered the sofa. This was to be my "casual" residence for most of the following three years and the three lads became some of my greatest friends. It wasn't long before I was being introduced to, and accepted, by their large circle of friends. I had certainly fallen on my feet.

***

The end of March arrived. Frontier had decided that all the new drivers should have a probationary trip as a co-driver, before attaining the status of a full driver/leader. I was to team up with Micky Hines on a two-week trip to Marrakesh. It was the first time that Frontier had attempted to complete this run in two weeks and as we set out, Micky was not happy with the situation. I was about to jump in at the deep end (not for the last time) and I had to learn to swim – and quickly!

We met, as was usual, at Victoria Station, got the 12 passengers organised and the roof rack packed, and set off for Dover to catch the evening crossing to Calais. Micky again began to interrogate me on the fact hat, although his and Gus's paths had crossed on several occasions the previous year, he couldn't remember seeing me. I again responded that I couldn't remember having seen him either. Micky kept giving me suspicious and slightly concerned sideways looks (something I was to get very accustomed to over the next couple of weeks), as if he was still trying to work out why we hadn't bumped into each other until now.

Landing in Calais about 12.30am, we began driving south. As per my trip with Safari, the usual routine on these trips was to drive straight through France overnight and through the next day, with the first stop scheduled for San Sebastian in the north of Spain. At about 3.00am Micky turned to me and asked if I could take the wheel for a while, as he was feeling tired and was going to grab a couple of hours sleep. He was still under the impression that I had been driving this route in similar vehicles for the last couple of years with Gus, while the truth of the matter was that this was the first time I had ever sat behind the wheel of a Ford Transit. This was only my second-ever trip abroad and although I was a better than average driver, I had never driven on the "wrong" side of the road before. So the Transit, with its full contingent of passengers and loaded roof rack, was a daunting prospect at that moment in time. It was pitch dark, pouring with rain and I had no idea where any of the controls were situated - I didn't even know how to turn off the windscreen wipers should it stop raining. I couldn't ask Micky about the controls without blowing my cover, so I sat there trying to compose myself and get my bearings. Micky asked me what I was waiting for so, trying not to panic, I asked him where we were headed. He gave me that look again. "Jaysus – you've done this trip before; Poitier, fecking Poitier - straight down the N fecking 10!" I explained, not very convincingly, that I was always a bit "rusty" at the beginning of a season, that Gus had done most of the driving when we were working together and that I hadn't taken much notice of the route! He gave me "the look" again and then promptly curled up on the front seat and went to sleep.

I set off very slowly, peering into the darkness and hoping that I would be able to comprehend the French road signs. Twelve passengers and their driver/leader slept on, blissfully unaware that they were in the hands of a complete novice. Micky woke just after dawn, looked around, asked where we were and gave me a rather sour, disdainful look before observing, "We haven't come very fecking far", when it transpired that we had covered just 60 miles in three hours. I mumbled an apology, conjuring up the excuse that I liked to take things slowly at the beginning of a trip and I didn't really like driving at night, especially when it was raining - and then went to sleep.

***

We journeyed through France and then down through Spain, where I had my first experience of mountain driving. I had grown in confidence as the journey progressed and felt competent in my handling of the Transit, so that by the time we reached the Sierra Nevada I was really settling into my role as an "overland driver". Driving down out of the mountains towards Malaga, I found myself negotiating a steep gradient and suddenly realised there was a sharp switch-back at the bottom of the slope. It was then that I discovered that the brakes on a Transit were not terribly efficient and had the tendency to fade when travelling downhill with 14 people and a fully laden roof rack. My foot was pumping at the brake pedal as I swung the steering wheel and we took the bend on two wheels. Micky was braced against the passenger door looking at me with a nervous, twitchy stare and, in a slightly trembling voice, enquired if I was "all right". I tried to compose myself and in the most casual tone I could muster, assured him that I was fine and everything was under control. We continued on our way to Marbella, which in 1970 was still just a small coastal town on the Costa-del-Sol, with Micky shooting nervous glances in my direction every few minutes. However, I had learnt a valuable lesson, one that would stand me in good stead in the future.

We spent that night on a beach campsite run by Julio, a recently acquired friend of Micky's. On our arrival, Micky indicated where the tents should be pitched and, leaving me to get things organised, announced that he could be found in the bar if needed. During the next couple of hours, I watched as he slowly demolished a litre bottle of Bacardi, thinly laced with cola, before he proceeded to curl up on a bench seat and fall asleep. He slept well that night.

The trip continued on into Morocco - Tangier, Meski, Fez, Marrakesh and back to Tangier. Micky was baffled by my lack of knowledge of the country. On arriving in Fez, he instructed me to take the passengers and drive them down to the kasbah while he sorted things out at the campsite reception, (for "campsite reception" read "bar"). I asked him for directions, as I couldn't "quite get my bearings". Micky gave me that uncomprehending look of his and informed me that it was "straight down the fecking road!" He seemed to be getting quite exasperated. By now I was wondering how long I could continue to pull the wool over his eyes.

It was while we were camping in Tangier on the return leg of the trip that I came face to face, as it were, with the carnal side of an overland driver's life. We had arrived in Tangier late in the evening and Micky had decided that we would camp rough on the beach between Tangier and Ceuta, which would enable us to catch the early ferry from Ceuta to Algeciras the next morning. It would also save Micky a night's campsite fees – all part of the perks of the job. I had decided to sleep in the Transit that night to avoid having to erect a tent, when the driver's door opened and Micky jumped into the front seat, closely followed by Janette, a young lady from the group. There followed a lot of whispering and giggling, before the minibus started rocking alarmingly from side to side. I lay there in a cold sweat, wondering whether I should announce my presence in a casually jocular manner, or remain "asleep", when the rocking suddenly stopped and I heard Janette ask Micky in a hoarse whisper whether I was in the bus. A head appeared over the back of the front seat and Micky replied that I was, but it was OK because I was asleep. My decision had been made for me! The rocking restarted and carried on for some time, accompanied by much gasping and heavy breathing, before the action finally ceased and the two of them departed as suddenly as they had arrived.

Four days later we were back in England. Micky presumably tendered a favourable report on me despite my shortcomings, as a week later I was told that I would be getting my own Transit and my first trip as a driver/leader would be down to Greece. My *own* Transit! A couple of weeks later, I stood there admiring my new pride and joy in her bright orange livery with the words "Frontier International" emblazoned in large white letters along the side. It was love at first sight!

My life was about to change dramatically; the overland years would prove to be the formative years for the rest of my life.

IT'S THE DOUBLE LIFE FOR STEVE

Steve Walker leads a double life. In winter he works as a telephone engineer. In summer it's following the sun as a travel firm's minibus driver.

This will be Steve's first summer with Frontier International, who run 24 minibuses throughout Europe. But he has had a lot of driving experience with another firm, Safari.

He became interested when he decided to have a holiday with Safari to Morocco. Steve says he caught the "travelling bug" on that trip and decided being a European driver was the life for him.

This year he has trips lined up to Morocco, Greece,

Turkey, India, Russia, and even the world famous Munich beer festival.

He begins work in April with a luxury trip to Morocco. For those who like the outdoor life. Steve of Marlborough Road, Brentwood, says these trips are just the thing.

Outdoor camping, with all equipment provided, is integrated with hotel stops.

To promote bookings, Steve has advertised in newspapers for "young mixed groups." But he added: "Young means anyone from about 18 to 30."

But it's not all hard work, said Steve: "It is a rough-it type of holiday—but great."

Aticle from the Brentwood Gazette 1970

4. SOLO

Now it's one thing to assist someone on a trip to Morocco, particularly when they are making all the decisions and you have at least visited the country before, but it's quite another thing to be let loose on the Continent with a brand-new bus full of passengers, not knowing how to get to where you're supposed to be taking them. A trip to Greece for my first solo run was a daunting prospect. First of all, where was Greece? In which direction did I point my Transit when I drove off the ferry in Zeebrugge? I began to wonder if I had bitten off more that I could chew, but there was no backing out now.

I arrived in Zeebrugge a week later at 5 am, with an early season compliment of just seven passengers and a feeling of trepidation. It had suddenly dawned on me during the channel crossing that I had never actually personally negotiated a customs post, let alone found my way to an unfamiliar, far-off country. I drove off the ferry trying desperately to remember what I had to do next, when I spotted an orange Transit in the queue of vehicles waiting to embark for the crossing to Dover, with Gus sitting behind the wheel. I have never felt more relieved to see someone! I ran over and questioned him about the Customs procedure and how to find my way from Zeebrugge to Greece. Gus sat there with a grin on his face, hugely enjoying my obvious panic and yet still looking somewhat self-satisfied at seeing his protégé taking their first steps as a fully-fledged driver.

He explained that I would need to buy Belgian road tax at the customs post before I left the docks. More panic! This hadn't been explained to me and there was nothing in my trip notes referring to this. I didn't have any Belgian francs, as I'd filled the petrol tank in Dover which would take me through to Germany and I hadn't envisage having to stop and pay for anything in Belgium. However, I was in luck; Gus had some spare francs that I could buy from him. He said I would need 250 francs for the tax and the same on the return trip. He asked me for £5 and handed over 500 francs. Relief! What a life-saver!

Now, which way to Greece? No problem, Gus assured me. I just had to drive out of the docks and pick up the E5 on the far side of the roundabout. That one road would take me all the way through Europe and on down to Greece. All I had to do was refer to the trip notes that I'd been given by Frontier and follow the road signs from one town to the next, as per the itinerary. Customs was no problem; I should collect the passports and hand them, together with the vehicle documents, to the customs officer who would stamp the passports and then direct me to the office where I could buy the road tax – all very simple and straight forward. Well, they say that a friend in need is a friend indeed – and I was certainly that at that moment in time!

I thanked Gus profusely, promising to stand him a large drink the next time we met up and, feeling very relieved and much more like the confident overland driver I was supposed to be, re-joined the passengers and drove up to the customs post. They took one look at us and waved us through. No passports required; no stamp; no road tax – they didn't even step out of their cosy little customs office! I drove out of the docks and picked up the E5.

I was very lucky on that maiden trip, having been blessed with an extremely understanding bunch of passengers. Deciding that honesty was the best policy under the circumstances and to come clean, I explained that this was my first solo trip and also my first to Greece. Taking this in their stride, they immediately offered to navigate for me and help with the general running of the trip. I will always be eternally grateful to that group; they truly helped me to come out of my shell and to begin to find my true self. In the next few years during my time as an overland driver it was to be proven time and time again that those groups who entered into the spirit of things and were prepared to pitch in and help with the day-to-day running of the trip had a much more enjoyable and satisfying experience than those that sat around waiting for everything to be done for them. There was nothing worse for me during those years on the road than waking up in the morning, having driven maybe ten or twelve hours the previous day and knowing you had maybe a similar drive ahead of you, to find your passengers sitting around the minibus with their suitcases and tents, waiting for "the driver" to climb up and load the roof rack. Some of these people wouldn't even bother to offer me breakfast. Fortunately, most groups would help to load the bus and would even, occasionally, bring me breakfast in bed!

The drive through Belgium took about four hours and we passed through the German border at Aachen with the minimum of fuss. My confidence was growing with each mile and I was beginning to feel the part when it suddenly dawned on me that Gus might have short-changed me. Back then exchange rates were fixed and most banks produced a card showing all the major currency rates. At the next "comfort break" I took the opportunity to check and sure enough my suspicions were confirmed; the rate for Belgian francs was 120 to the pound sterling, not 100; as I was being paid the grand sum of £14 a week, the difference, for me, was quite substantial!

***

We camped that night in the cathedral city of Cologne; the following day, driving down the autobahn towards Frankfurt, I saw an orange Transit approaching on the opposite side of the road, flashing its lights. I flashed my lights in response and pulled over onto the hard shoulder, before leaping out of my seat and dodging across the carriageway. I had seen this scenario acted out several times on my two Moroccan trips – the screeching to a halt, the joyful camaraderie of the two drivers and the exchange of banter between two "knights of the road"! To my amazement the other bus was being driven by Micky Hynes; instead of a friendly greeting, he said how relieved he was to see another Frontier bus and asked how much money I had with me. Feeling somewhat disappointed and deflated, I replied that I just had my trip funds.

Micky swore, "They only gave me £140 for the trip down to Greece and now I'm skint. Jeysus that Greece is an expensive place – I'm not going back there again in a hurry; I'll stick with Morocco. I've been borrowing money from the passengers since Austria and now they're completely spent out. I'm nearly out of petrol and I've got to make the ferry at Zeebrugge by tomorrow morning. So, how much can you lend me?"

Now this was not very encouraging for a novice driver, particularly as Micky, an experienced driver, had been given £20 more than me for his trip and had run out of money. The only thing I had in my favour was that I only had seven passengers, as opposed to his ten, so I should at least be able to save a bit on campsite fees. I explained that I had only been given £120 and at a stretch could let him have £10.

"Is that all?" pleaded Micky. I pointed out that I had started out with £20 less than him and that I dare not give him any more in case I had any emergencies during the trip. After some deliberation he grudgingly accepted that £10 was better than nothing, took the money and with no further ado, jumped back into his bus and took off in the direction of Belgium. So much for the "joyful camaraderie and friendly banter"!

We camped overnight in Munich and left early the next morning, thankful for a good night's sleep. The scenery was breath-taking as we drove through the Bavarian Alps and on into Austria. We passed through Saltzburg and couldn't believe how clean and tidy the town was, which proved to be a feature of Austria as a whole. It was a beautiful country, with its traditional wooden chalets, the rugged snow-capped mountains rising around them and the lower slopes consisting of fertile meadows full of wild flowers. We stopped overnight in Graz, travelling on the next day into Yugoslavia.

My initial impressions on my first visit to a communist country lived up to my expectations; the customs officers were sullen and the entry procedures were long-winded. Once we got under way, Northern Yugoslavia appeared to be reasonably prosperous as we drove through an area of ski resorts on our way to Maribor and on to Zagreb. However, the autoput between Zagreb and Belgrade, a distance of some 200 miles, was the worst stretch of road I ever encountered and probably the worst in Europe. It consisted of a three-lane highway, a lane in each direction and a common overtaking lane down the centre, carrying a high volume of traffic as it was the main artery between Western Europe and Asia. The road was straight and flat, with no towns or villages, just the occasional service station where the lorry drivers would stop for a coffee and a slivovitz. It was flanked on either side with fields of maize and, in one section, a large forest of fir trees; it was full of potholes and very boring. I had been driving the forested stretch for about an hour when I started to nod off. I woke with a start with the minibus wandering across the road. It never happened again. The Yugoslavs had a tradition of marking the location of fatal road accidents with a wreath at the side of the road. Every accident I ever saw on that stretch of road had a lorry involved and the roadside for the whole 200 miles was littered with wreaths.

That night we stayed on the municipal campsite in Belgrade, a cheerless place, before moving quickly on the next day to Nis, Skopje and eventually the Greek border. The road improved dramatically after Belgrade, both in quality and scenery. A dual carriageway cut its way through majestic mountains and ran alongside spectacular gorges on its way south. On subsequent trips I often drove non-stop through Yugoslavia, driving through the day and on through the night; as long as the passengers were agreeable, we would make up an extra day which could then be spent on the beach in Greece - and I would save a night's campsite fees!

Driving overnight to make up an extra day would become a regular occurrence on future trips. It was a challenge that required unfaltering concentration over long, lonely hours at the wheel while the passengers slept. It was just me, the Transit - and the road. I was a smoker back then and it broke the monotony to reach for the packet of cigarettes on top of the dashboard, take one out, light it and smoke it. This became almost a ritual that helped to concentrate the mind as mile after mile slipped by. The drive down to Greece was scheduled to take four days, but with an overnight drive through Yugoslavia and a tail wind, you could make it in three. I found that, gradually, these drives toughened me as a person, giving me an inner strength and a belief in my own capabilities. I felt invulnerable – that I could drive forever. Then at the end of each drive, I felt the warm, satisfying glow of achievement – and I felt alive.

***

After the dour experience of Yugoslavia Greece was a haven of friendliness, smiles and hospitality. The customs officers were good natured; on discovering that we were English, they only wanted to talk about football and "Bobby Charlton". We eventually got away and stopped ten miles down the road in a small town by the name of Polykastron, where we decided to take refreshments. We entered the first taverna we came to and were met by the proprietor who introduced himself as Aris. He sat us all down, supervised the serving of drinks and then left us, re-appearing a few minutes later sporting a bouzouki, a traditional Greek instrument similar to a lute that produces a sharp metallic sound, reminiscent of a mandolin. It transpired that Aris had played bouzouki professionally on cruise ships and all over Europe, before returning to Polykastron and opening his taverna.

He proceeded to provide us with an unforgettable evening of traditional music, encouraging several of the local clientele to contribute to the entertainment with an impromptu display of Greek dancing as the music worked its magic. They say first impressions count and I could not have had a better introduction to Greece and its people. It was love at first sight and the beginning of a lifelong association with the country and its people. Aris's taverna became a regular stop on future trips and his welcome always had a magical effect on my passengers.

After staying longer than intended – something that proved to be a common occurrence when we stopped at Aris's, we drove east along the north coast to Kavala, a beautiful town situated mid-way between Thessalonika and Turkey and the birthplace of Muhammad Ali Pasha al-Mas'ud ibn Agha, also known as Muhammad Ali of Egypt and the Sudan, considered to be the founder of modern Egypt. We continued on to the tiny fishing village of Heraclizia some 10km west of Kavala, along a cliff-top road which stopped abruptly when it reached the village. Frontier had established an unofficial campsite on a small headland shaded by pine trees, overlooking a bay with a stunning sandy beach – and George's taverna. This was not the Greece that the average tourist saw; this was the real Greece. It was here that I fell instantly in love with the country, the way the people enjoyed the simple pleasures of life to the full – the sun, the sea, their food, their music and their dancing. The village had one small general store, two tavernas, George's on the beach and Theo's in the village square - and perfect tranquillity. Breakfast in either taverna consisted of a plate of fried eggs swimming in the local green olive oil, with chips and the compulsory village bread.

It was here that I met Roy Williams, a large, gentle man who looked a bit like Joe Cocker (and did quite a fair impression of him singing "With a Little Help from My Friends"). He came to the village every year to spend the summer living on the beach. Roy was a great character who spoke with a stammer until he'd had a few beverages - after which the stammer magically disappeared. Most of the time he spent in Heraclizia he spoke without a stammer. Although his parents were Welsh, he had a large repertoire of Irish rebel songs that he would entertain us with on nights when the drinks were flowing freely – which was basically every night. He had been joined in the village that summer by Peter Fischer and his girlfriend Tebbi. They were American hippies who had been travelling round Europe, had found the village and had decided to spend the summer there, pitching their tent in a small bay on the far side of the main beach and living mainly on local fruit, vegetables and salads. I always looked forward to the company of these three whenever I stayed in the village, feeling privileged to enjoy their friendship, humour and freedom of spirit; they were people of the time.

***

After three glorious days we drove back through Thessaloniki and then south to Platamon, a small town sitting below Mount Olympus, where we stopped at Castle Camping, which derived its name from a 14th century fortress on the outskirts of the town, and was situated on a beach that was a vast expanse of golden sand. I was sitting in the toilet one evening, as you do, when I had the distinct and uncomfortable feeling that I was being watched. Looking around I spotted a small, bright green tree frog attached to the wall. I later discovered that the area around Platamon was blessed with its own micro-climate, which was almost sub-tropical in the summer.

The next day, we decided to relax on the beach, as the crystal clear and stunningly blue Aegean looked so inviting and there was a volley ball net on the beach. One of my passengers, Derek, was a bachelor in his early forties who came from Highbury in London and worked for a small family concern that made billiard tables. He was a quiet man who saved his money in order to go off on holiday to a different country each year; the previous year he had been on a trip to Russia. On this particular morning he told me he couldn't swim and was not a beach person; consequently, he had decided to go walking up in the foothills of Olympus behind the town.

The rest of us spent the day swimming, playing volley ball and doing beach-type things. That evening, as dusk fell and we were gathering in the campsite restaurant, I suddenly realised that we were missing Derek. No one had seen him all day. It gets dark very quickly in Greece and I was beginning to panic, having visions of calling out the local police to form a search party. My first solo trip – and I had lost a passenger! At around 8.30 that evening Derek wandered into the campsite looking, for all the world, like a schoolboy who had been "scrumping" in someone's orchard. He was clutching his hat in his hands;, both the hat and his pockets were overflowing with huge, dark red cherries. He sat down looking somewhat confused at all the fuss as we gathered round to ask where he had been. After leaving us that morning he had walked up into the hills and, after an hour or so, had met a local farmer. Although neither of them spoke a word of the other's language, they had become involved in a long, drawn-out conversation with the help of much animated sign language. The farmer wanted to know where Derek was from and what he did for a living. They conversed in this manner for some time, until the farmer eventually invited Derek back to his farm for something to eat and drink. He was introduced to the farmer's wife, before the three of them sat down at a table laden with food and wine, to share a leisurely and sumptuous meal of local dishes. After an afternoon siesta on the veranda, they took a stroll around the farm and Derek was loaded up with cherries from the orchard. It had been difficult to drag himself away, but eventually he had said his goodbyes and, after promising to send copies of the photographs he had taken, made his way back to the campsite. I was amazed that two complete strangers, who didn't speak each-others language, could spend a whole day conversing and forging a friendship.

On leaving Platamon the following morning, we headed south along the National Highway towards Athens. According to my trusty trip notes there was a campsite to the west of the city, situated on a beach in the vicinity of Daphni. It was run by a Brit and had a restaurant, bar and swimming pool. It was a long, hot drive to Athens, broken up by frequent stops for refreshment at the roadside cafés. During my time in Greece I quickly became addicted to *rizogalo*, a cold rice pudding, that was always available in these establishments and was both nourishing and remarkably refreshing. At times, I virtually lived on the stuff!

After a full day's drive, we arrived on the outskirts of Athens and eventually found our way to the designated campsite. It was a disaster! The place was, to say the least, ramshackle, and it was situated next to an oil refinery. The "swimming pool" was a metal tank some six feet high by twenty feet square full of slimy, green water, while the "beach" consisted of oil-covered rocks. We took one look at it and left, much to the annoyance of the proprietor, who looked like a retired army major in his late sixties. He was most indignant and shouted something about suing us, as he had a contract with the company.

It was unanimously agreed that we should have a look at a campsite we had passed a couple of miles back in Daphni, which was used by most of the other overland companies. However, it was an overcrowded dust bowl; we gave it one look and departed. In desperation we decided to check out one last place that we had spotted on the northern outskirts of Athens at Kifissia. Thankfully, Camping Nea Kifissia was a joy. It was set in a grove of fir trees on the edge of a small valley. It also had a proper swimming pool that was immaculately clean. There was a nightclub and restaurant on site which was frequented by young Athenians, especially at weekends when the place was packed out. The whole setup was run by George Komianidis, a sophisticated, well-educated man in his early fifties.

***

I was the first overland driver to use Nea Kifissia, something that George never forgot; many drivers followed me there over the next couple of years, during which time it became "the" campsite to use in Athens. George took on the role of father figure to the drivers and was always ready to help with any problems that might occur. The nightclub had been, and continued to be, the launch pad for many of the country's top singers such as Yiannis Poloupolous, the Greek equivalent of Tom Jones. George was quick to realise that the overland groups made up of young Brits, Aussies, Kiwis, etc. provided an attraction for his nightclub clientele, so campers enjoyed concessionary prices in the restaurant and bar, while drivers ate and drank free of charge.

Often, late on a Saturday night when things were winding down in the club, George would gather up a couple of drivers together with their girlfriends, and drive to Glyfada in the south of Athens, to one of the top *bouzoukia* – nightclubs that featured popular Greek music. He would settle us at a table and proceed to order drinks and snacks. We must have looked a strange sight, as the table would often consist of an odd collection of hairy hippies and some of George's friends who were generally rather well-dressed Athenians. Flower sellers would wander from table to table with their baskets full of gardenias which you could buy to throw at a favourite singer. George wouldn't mess around; he would buy a whole basketful and present the women on our table with the flowers, accompanied by a kiss of their hand. He was charm personified, but sincere and not at all phoney. He would throw the remaining gardenias in handfuls at the singers, most of whom he seemed to know personally. We would often end up having breakfast at about 6.00am in the Plaka area of the city, before heading back to the campsite to grab a couple of hours sleep under canvas.

We spent three days in Athens doing all the usual things – visiting the Akropolis, museums, the Plaka and Mount Lycabettus with its funicular railway and its unparalleled view out over the city and down to the port of Piraeus and the bay of Faliro. It was a city that I found charming, but at the same time frustrating. I loved the individuality of each area of the city; the old-world grandeur of Syntagma Square with its grand hotels and Parliament, complete with its guard of *Evzoni*, the cheap gloss and glamour of Omonia Square and its street cafés, cut-price shops and attendant red-light area and the timeless quality of the Plaka spreading up the hillside beneath the Akropolis. However, the city traffic was noisy and belligerent, often coming to a complete standstill amid a cacophony of car horns and rising tempers.

On the first day there, I was looking for a retreat from the heat of the day while my group visited the Akropolis – something I had decided could wait until it was a little cooler, when I stumbled upon a small art gallery just below the monument, run by an English couple who showed me around and provided me with refreshments. On future trips, I was to spend many cool, pleasant hours sitting in the gallery sipping wine, chatting and enjoying their company.

The final evening in Athens was spent discovering the thrills of what I believe was the country's one and only horse racing track, at Faliro. These evening meetings were held under floodlights and consisted of sprints over 800 hundred and 1,000 metres. The betting was government controlled, and was based on a fixed-odds system. We were constantly bombarded with tips and advice from the local punters who would, if their horse won, present themselves, wreathed in smiles, to declare that they knew all there was to know about horses and horse racing, while the unsuccessful tipsters would mysteriously disappear. We had a thoroughly enjoyable time and I ended up about 35 drachma (around 50p) up on the evening.

On leaving Athens we retraced our steps, heading north up the National Highway to Lamia where we took the inland route through the mountains to Larissa. From there we turned due west, travelling across the Plain of Thessaly, a rich fertile area of cotton and maize fields, cattle and flocks of geese. As we neared Trikala, we turned north-west towards Kalambaka and were stunned by the sight of immense pillars of rock, huge monoliths, rising from the flatlands and reaching for the sky. Drawing closer we could see buildings perched on top of some of them, while others appeared to be clinging to the sheer rock face - we were approaching Meteora and its attendant monasteries. There was a homely little campsite just below Meteor; the next morning we were able to drive up a narrow winding road to one of the larger monasteries, taking in the breath-taking view across the plain while eagles soared around the rocky crags. Some of the smaller monasteries were only accessible by rope and basket, deliveries of both provisions and new recruits being made by this method. That afternoon we drove back across the plain to spend another night at Platamon, our last night in Greece before our return trip through Europe.

We arrived back in England on the Sunday afternoon and drove from Dover to London stuck behind the inevitable "Sunday afternoon drivers", but somehow it didn't matter. The trip had been a great success all round, due in no small part to my happy bunch of passengers. I couldn't have had a better group for my inauguration on my first solo trip as an overland driver. I had arrived back with the grand sum of £15 in hand from my trip funds, despite the "loan" that I had donated to Micky Hines. I discovered some time later that Micky had spent quite a large proportion of his trip funds in Heraclizia drinking the local spumante that came in half-litre, crown-top bottles at the princely sum of 5 drachma; at that time there were 70 drachma to the pound, so I can only imagine how many bottles/crates of the stuff he had managed to imbibe!

I returned from that trip more confident, more assured and a very different person from the one that had left Dover two weeks earlier. I was beginning to find my true self.

5. SUMMER

I spent a week in the office at Crawley being teased about the exchange rate for Belgian francs, Gus having wasted no time in taking great delight relating to the entire office staff how he had short-changed me! My next assignment was a three-week trip to Turkey – another new and exciting experience in the waiting. The itinerary took us down through Europe on the same route as the previous trip to Greece, until we reached Nis in Yugoslavia, when we headed for the Bulgarian border. Negotiating this border proved to be something of a trial. We needed visas in order to enter the country, there being two types. The visitor's visa cost the equivalent of 75p, while the transit visa was £1.50. If you took the cheaper visitor's visa you were required to stay in the country for a minimum of three days and spend at least the minimum stipulated amount of money. To ensure that you did spend the money each person had to change a minimum amount into Bulgarian Levs – the closest thing to Monopoly money that I had encountered, which was worthless outside Bulgaria and virtually impossible to change back into sterling, or any other currency for that matter. It was a pretty neat set-up from the perspective of the Bulgarian treasury and its tourist industry!

We stayed the night at a campsite outside Plovdiv before travelling on the next day to the Turkish border at Edirne. Having eventually negotiated the Bulgarian customs we entered

Turkey and drove the 150 miles to Istanbul, stopping some 10 miles short of the city at the splendid Camping Londra. I was captivated by the vast, expansive fields of sunflowers flanking the road on the way, their huge yellow heads all facing towards the sun and standing in orderly rows as far as the eye could see.

The next morning, we headed for the city and the Grand Bazaar, one of the largest and oldest covered markets in the world. It was built in 1461 and had over 4,000 shops selling virtually anything you could imagine. On the trip down through Europe I had met Tony, a Scotsman who imported leather garments from Turkey into the UK, and had recommended a shop located in the bazaar that he did business with. The bazaar presented a head-turning array of beautiful gold and silver jewellery, brightly coloured carpets and kilims, stylish leather jackets and Afghan coats and of course the famous puzzle rings. Having located the shop Tony had spoken about, I introduced myself to the owner, Mustafa Kasapoglu, explaining that I and other Frontier drivers would be regular visitors to Istanbul throughout the year. Mustafa was a well-educated man, who had a Yugoslav father and Romanian mother, but had been born and raised in Turkey and had been an officer in the Turkish army during the Korean War.

His shop set-up was impressive. It became standard procedure for me to take my passengers to Mustafa's on our first morning in the city, to get measured up for leather jackets, trousers and coats which would be made-to-measure in 24 hours for the princely sum of £10. When their purchases had been made the group would go off for the day with a guide, Oran who was employed by Mustafa, to visit the puzzle ring factory before going on to the Blue Mosque, St. Sofia and the Topkapi Palace. Meanwhile, after taking the Transit to a car park behind the bazaar where two boys would clean it inside and out for about 25p, I would spend the day relaxing in the shop enjoying what was effectively a day of rest, chatting to Mustafa's customers and practising my sales technique on them. One of the shop boys would be despatched periodically throughout the day to fetch sweet corn from street-corner vendors with large boilers full of succulent cobs, or small plates of delicious meatballs from the iconic Pudding Shop, together with beer, Coke or small glasses of sweet black tea.

Oran would return with the group around four in the afternoon. After they had all been treated to drinks by Mustafa, who was well versed in public relations, we returned to the campsite to get cleaned and changed in readiness for the evening's entertainment – organised by Mustafa. We would drive back into town at about 6.30 and pick up Oran who would then direct us to one of the many small fish restaurants along the Bosporus, to the north of the city, where we would rendezvous with Mustafa. A typical three course meal would be laid on, after which we would depart for a nightclub, usually at the Hilton, where we would be entertained by a cabaret of exotic traditional belly dancers. From there we moved on to Taxim Square to spend the rest of the evening in one of the surprisingly good discos, arriving back at the campsite at around three or four in the morning.

The next day was a "free" day for my passengers, allowing them to explore the city at their leisure before collecting their leather gear which was waiting for them at Mustafa's shop later that afternoon. After delivering them back to the campsite, I would then drive back to the city, often accompanied by a couple of young ladies from the group, to meet up with Mustafa, who would then take us to an area about 10km north of the city where some of the best restaurants in Turkey could be found situated on jetties built out over the Bosporus. We would be treated to a sumptuous meal comprising of six or seven courses spread out over the next three or four hours. I remember on one occasion watching the waiter open a trapdoor in the jetty floor to haul up an enormous lobster that had been tethered on a length of rope. It was despatched to the kitchen and then presented steaming hot about half an hour later to the lucky recipients. It was always a pleasure to be in Istanbul and, thanks to Mustafa, it became a haven of relaxation for me whenever I stayed there.

*

First Class Leather and
Suede Garments

Erstklassige Leder und
Wildlederbekleidung

Confezioni di Pelle e di
Renna di prima Quâlità

Vêtements de première
Qualité en Cuir
et en Daim

*

Mustafa Kasapoğlu

Divanyolu, Adliye Karşısı Işık Sokak Ören Han No. 12-14

TELEPHONES   OFFICE : 26 34 41   İSTANBUL — TURKEY
              HOME : 46 35 42

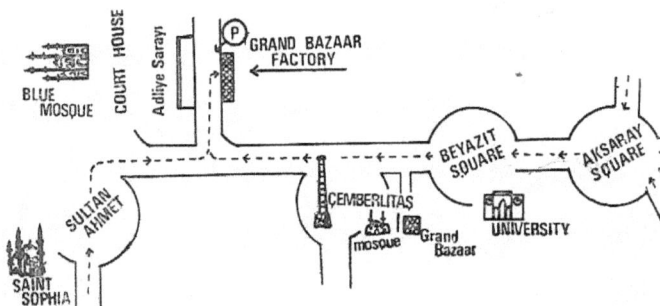

Mustafa's business card

***

On leaving the European side of Istanbul we took the ferry across the Bosporus and into Asia. The ferry was filled to the gunnels with people and their belongings, including goats, chickens and some geese. It was only a fifteen-minute crossing and was one of the cheapest ferries I ever encountered, costing just 50p for the minibus and 5p for each passenger. We travelled down to the south coast, visiting Bursa, Izmir and Ephesus, before driving up the west coast, stopping at Troy on the way to Canakkale. There wasn't a lot to see at Troy, but I did come across probably the best rip-off of all time there. A small man had set up a stall at the entrance to the site with a large basket full of fresh-looking wood chippings and a sign pronouncing these as being pieces of the actual wooden horse, available to buy at the knock-down price of one dollar each! I don't know how many he managed to sell, but I had to give him full marks for enterprise

We boarded a ferry at Canakkale to take us across the Dardenelles and back to Europe. Crossing the River Evros into Greece we moved on to Heraclizia, where we found Roy Williams in "residence" with a group of his friends who got together whenever possible. They consisted of Stu Sissons (The Wolf) who was an "occasional" overland driver, Robin (Rabbit), a scouser with a brilliant sense of humour, Rabbit's girlfriend Sue (Piglet) and Willard (The Rat). For some obscure reason, (or maybe no reason at all), I became known as "The Goat". I was to discover that whenever this crowd got together, it was going to be an entertaining experience!

Later that summer, I suggested we all get together at the campsite in Nea Kifissia. Roy had put together a "skiffle" instrument that he named Oscar. Oscar consisted of a broom handle with an old boot nailed to the bottom, a piece of tin plate attached halfway up and about a dozen nails with three or four crown bottle tops on each one, hammered into the top half. Roy would get a rhythm going, stomping the boot on the ground which got the bottle tops rattling, and then creating a sub-rhythm by hitting the tin plate with an empty beer bottle. The whole effect was highly entertaining; once when Komianidis saw Roy and Oscar in full flow, he immediately gave him a slot on stage every night at the night club.

Sitting beside the campsite swimming pool one afternoon, Stu suggested we should have an underwater drinking contest. We all sat on the edge of the pool, each holding a bottle of beer with our thumb over the top; on the count of three we jumped into the pool, sinking to the bottom and trying to drink as much as we could before closing the bottle with our thumb again and heading back to the surface – the winner, obviously, being the one who had drunk the most. It made for a great afternoon.

***

In August, I had a group of mainly Americans; having spent a couple days in Platamon we were driving down the main highway to Athens (not the most interesting road – particularly when you've done it a few times). It was mid-summer, the heat was oppressive and most of the passengers had dozed off as we approached the site of the Battle of Thermopylae which was now just a parking area set off the highway featuring a memorial to the brave Spartans who had fought in the famous battle against the might of the Persian army. It consisted of a large, impressive statue of Leonidis, the Spartan king, holding a spear and naked apart from his battle helmet. Greek signs were, of course, written in Greek, but also – particularly in tourist areas, in phonetic

English. In this case, the English version of "Thermopylae" had been written as "THERMOPILE". Having driven for a few hours on what was, for me, a pretty boring journey I decided, on the spur of the moment, to have a bit of fun.

As we pulled into the parking area, the passengers began to wake up; while they were still in a state of drowsiness, I explained that this was a statue to commemorate an ancient Greek doctor who had invented a cure for haemorrhoids using a thermic lance – hence the name THERMO PILE. I told them that this was a statue of the said doctor holding his thermic lance. The passengers, bless them, took this all in and proceeded to take the compulsory photos, before we continued on our journey.

I would like to beg forgiveness from those passengers (and their children and children's children who may have had the story told to them – possibly with the accompanying photos), and who may even still believe that there is a Greek statue of an ancient doctor who invented a cure for haemorrhoids.

***

Leaving Greece was always a wrench, as I was faced with the drive through Yugoslavia and the daunting prospect of "Death Valley" – the stretch of road between Belgrade and Zagreb. On some trips, having survived the journey to Zagreb we would be scheduled to travel south through the mountains to Rijeka, then along the coast to the Italian border at Trieste and on to Venice, skirting the industrial area at Mestre and passing through the small village of Mal Contenta to the edge of the lagoon and Camping Fusina.

This was not your bog-standard European campsite. It was run by Renato Rossi, a large, friendly man in his mid-thirties. He and his lovely wife Maria had five young children and adopted any overland driver who used the campsite as one of the family. The bar was the focal point of the campsite; the walls were covered in graffiti, as every visiting overland group added its own contribution to the décor. Evenings spent at Fusina consisted of an outrageous frenzy of drinking, singing and dancing, stretching inevitably into the early hours of the morning. Proceedings would commence quite sedately, with Renato quietly strumming his guitar and a few of the local lads from the village joining in with some of their favourite arias. After a while as the drinks began to flow, the tempo would start to quicken until the gathering was in full song; eventually Renato would break into his repertoire of rugby songs. He knew every rugby song in the book; indeed, he taught me a few during my stays at Fusina. The bar was quite often "staffed" by one of the drivers who, as the evening progressed, would not be too careful when it came to serving up the drinks; by the end of the night the floor was usually awash with beer and wine. Breakfast was generally not a well-attended meal at Fusina. Family campers were not encouraged to stay; any arriving at the gate being advised, and encouraged, to find an alternative campsite, as things tended to be very noisy at night and it went on into the early hours. Very few decided to stay.

A boat ran each morning across the lagoon to Venice, stopping at one of the famous glass factories en route. This gave me a free day to relax on the campsite before driving over the causeway to collect the group in the evening. Maria would come searching for me around midday, so I could join the family for lunch. Maria, Renato and their children would be joined by the campsite staff and any drivers on site, all sitting down, as a family, to eat together. It was always a very warm, homely occasion and much appreciated when you had spent months at a time on the road.

If requested, Renato would organise a barbeque for a group during their stay at Fusina. Towards the end of that summer, I arrived at the campsite and, not realising it was a Sunday (I did occasionally lose track of time when on the road), asked if we could have a barbeque that evening. Renato explained that, as it was Sunday, the shops, including the butcher's, would be closed. However, undaunted he ushered me into his car and drove the 2km to Malcontenta. Arriving at the butcher's house mid-afternoon during the sacred siesta time, Renato proceeded to sound the car horn until a sleepy and dishevelled butcher appeared on the balcony in his underwear. After an exchange of words, the disgruntled tradesman was persuaded to drive with us to his shop, open the cold room and cut a dozen steaks from a side of beef hand-picked by Renato. That evening the group prepared a salad while Renato proceeded to cook the steaks over a large bed of charcoal; the barbeque was damped down with copious quantities of the inexpensive local white wine. At the end of a grand evening Renato refused to let me pay for the meal, saying that I had been a good customer and friend throughout the summer and the meal had been a "thank you" from him.

6. BACK TO GREECE

Over the following three months, I was gainfully employed, making several more trips to Greece and Turkey. At the end of August, I arrived in Zeebrugge on my return from a trip to Turkey to find a company courier waiting for me at the ferry terminal. There had been a problem with the ferry bookings and my next group, who were bound for Greece, were arriving as foot passengers that evening in Calais. I handed over my current group to the courier, bade them farewell and set off for Calais. Having just driven overnight from Innsbruck I didn't relish the thought of another two hours of driving and decided to grab a few hours sleep in the minibus before making my way to Calais. However, I woke up later than intended, necessitating a mad dash for the ferry. I arrived just as it was docking. It was raining as my new group made their way towards the minibus; when they were fully assembled, I discovered that I had a full complement of 14 passengers comprising of 13 women and one man - who was travelling with his fiancée. I had a feeling that this could be a difficult trip; three weeks to Greece and back with this group could have its problems.

We set off through Calais heading back towards Belgium; we had only been travelling for about ten minutes when someone called out from the back to say that one of the women had fainted. Reacting in true "overland driver" style I pulled in to the side of the road directly outside a café/bar, jumped out and ran inside, to emerge a few minutes later with a brandy and a black coffee. I had seen this scenario many times in the movies - lady in distress and macho man comes to her rescue! I offered the semi-conscious lady the brandy. She looked up and murmured that she didn't drink brandy. Oh well, you can't win them all. Instead, I offered her the coffee. She looked up again and murmured that she didn't drink coffee either! We sat her by the open door; after five or ten minutes she seemed to be a little better.I came to the conclusion that, since we had all the windows closed as it was raining, with 15 bodies crammed into the bus it had probably been a bit hot and stuffy inside.

We continued up to the Belgian border and then drove all that night and the following day through Belgium and Germany, eventually stopping in Munich that evening. During that time Rachel, our fainting lady, had spent about 60 percent of the journey in an unconscious or semi-conscious state; although she had a travelling companion, Jenny, who was looking after her, I was beginning to get just a little worried. Another member of the group was a German lady, Hannah. I asked if we could take Rachel to a doctor to check whether she was well enough to continue on the trip, and Hannah arranged for an examination the following morning. The doctor pronounced her physically fit and in no danger in that respect as far as the onward journey was concerned, but did add that he considered her to be in a state of mental exhaustion and it might not be a good idea for her to continue. I put this to Rachel and offered to arrange for her to return to the UK, but she was adamant that she wanted to see Greece, so we decided to continue with the trip as planned and review the situation on a day-to-day basis.

The next day we continued on into Austria and stopped that evening at Camping West in Graz, in the south of the country. It was an excellent campsite, with good facilities and plenty of space; it had become one of my favourite stop-overs. Just along the road from the campsite was a small bar/restaurant run by a diminutive woman and her daughter. It was very convenient and although the menu was limited – basically wiener schnitzel with salad, or goulash soup – it was excellent value, with both dishes costing thirty schillings (approximately 50p), while a half litre of very drinkable draught beer was six schillings. Having made our way there we were greeted by a friendly smile from our hostess who recognised me from my previous visits. We sat down, ordered our food and drinks and began to relax. A little later, as we began tucking into our meal, a huge two litre stein of beer was suddenly thumped onto the table in front of me, which I thought was a little odd, as I hadn't ordered it - in fact I had been quietly sipping my usual half litre at the time. I looked round to explain that there had been a mistake, to find our hostess with a big smile on her face, nodding vigorously and gesturing that this was on the house. I thanked her profusely, but realising that there was no way I could drink the two litres by myself, I took a big swig and then passed it round the table. After five minutes and two full circuits of the table we had just about polished it off and I sat back somewhat relieved. Within a couple of minutes, a second stein was placed in front of me. Our hostess was smiling and nodding again. This hospitable gesture was repeated on every subsequent visit that I made to this hostelry and was always well received by my passengers.

Crossing into Yugoslavia the next day, we travelled down the autoput to Belgrade where I decided to stay the night at the city's campsite rather than drive overnight, in case it had an adverse effect on Rachel. As dusk fell, one of the women came to tell me that Rachel had gone missing, so getting everyone together I organised a search and 20 minutes later she was found unconscious behind the shower block. We took her back to the bus and after reviving her, discovered that she had got lost on her way to the showers, panicked and blacked out. This was all getting quite worrying for me and the group, so I took Jenny, Rachel's travelling companion, to one side; after some persistent questioning she revealed that Rachel was in fact a manic depressive and was having treatment from a doctor who had recommended that she take a holiday. It transpired that, as a teenager, she had suffered an acid attack from a group of boys and was still suffering from the mental trauma it had caused. She had eventually (perhaps unwisely?) taken a job as a teacher which she naturally found very stressful under the circumstances. Having taken her doctor's advice, the holiday she had chosen was probably one of the most demanding holidays she possibly could have. Apparently, she had always had an ambition to see Greece and an overland trip was the only affordable way she could get there. Having heard that, I was now determined that she should realise her ambition and see the country in all its glory.

I was sitting in the minibus after this little episode when I was joined by Hannah who was like a reincarnation of Marlene Dietrich – tall and slim, with blonde hair, ice-blue eyes, and striking good looks, with an air of mystery about her. I had cast an occasional admiring glance in her direction over the previous couple of days, but had had no response. We talked for a while and I eventually suggested, quite casually that, as it was quite a chilly night, we might share a tent. The offer was graciously declined.

***

The following day we drove on to the Greek border at Evzoni and after the usual good-natured formalities which inevitably revolved around football and Bobby Charlton, we made our way down the road to Polykastron and Aris's taverna. Aris's face broke into a wide smile of welcome – much wider than usual as he watched my thirteen young ladies enter his premises. The bouzouki appeared along with the wine and the tensions of the previous three days quickly evaporated. I normally spent an hour or so at Aris's before moving on to Platamon, but on this particular evening we became captivated with soldiers from the local barracks engaging in traditional dances to the music. They had to be back in barracks by 10.00pm, so they all left, very reluctantly, except for one - Stratos, who had been taken by the music and a little too much ouzo. Aris was playing rembetika – a traditional music often referred to as Greek blues and which has a haunting, soul-searching quality to it. Stratos got up and started to dance zeibekiko, a dance that originated in the Aegean region of the Ottoman Empire. It had originally involved two armed men facing one another, but had evolved into an improvised dance for a single male. Zeibekiko has no set steps, but consists of improvised circular movements usually in a small, confined area. As he slowly circled, Stratos took a small ouzo glass from a table and, placing it on the floor, continued to dance round it making sweeping arm movements. Then, standing on one leg, he bent over and placed an index finger on the rim of the glass, pressing down on it until the glass shattered. He stood back up and continued to dance with a beatific smile on his face, grinding the fragments of glass into the floor under his heavy army boots.

I managed to drag the group away at about 10.30 that evening, three hours after we had arrived, and I still had a two-and-a-half-hour drive ahead of me. Most of the passengers were, needless to say, a bit worse for wear, having hit the ouzo and retsina with an alarming lack of restraint. After wending their way back to the Transit, they proceeded to collapse into their seats and fall asleep. As I pulled away from the taverna I was aware of someone resting their head on the back of my seat and realized that it was Hannah. A few minutes later I felt a kiss on the back of my neck and nearly drove off the road as a caressing hand slid round the side of my seat! Hannah obviously didn't beat about the bush once she had made her mind up! I don't think I ever drove the 100 miles between Polykastron and Platamon faster than I did that particular night and, on reaching the campsite, my tent went up in record time. That night I fell hopelessly in love with Hannah Schmidt.

We spent a couple of days on the beach at Platamon to enable everyone to recover from the trip down, before moving on to Athens. Rachel had improved immensely since arriving in Greece and actually seemed to be enjoying herself. Maybe it was travelling in foreign parts with a group of strangers, but there was something about overland trips that made people shed their inhibitions and really open up to reveal their true character after a few days together.

***

After our stay in Athens, we journeyed north to Meteora and then on to Heraclizia where I found Colin Payten in residence, together with his younger brother Barry and the company photographers, Caroline and Ted. We had a great time the following day, posing for photos for the 1971 Frontier

International brochure in which my group eventually featured quite heavily and I appeared on the front cover. That evening we were all congregated at George's taverna on the beach when an electric storm erupted in the mountains and a strong wind blew through the village. We sat watching the spectacle of mother nature stretching her muscles when one of the local lads came running down from the camping area up on the headland, shouting that several of the tents had been blown down. Rachel, who had been sitting and relaxing with the rest of us, promptly fell off her chair in a dead faint. We were so accustomed to this by now that nobody took any notice. However, George's wife and his elderly mother came rushing from the kitchen and began to fuss over Rachel like two old mother hens. Clothes were loosened, cold water administered to chest and forehead and smelling salts were fetched, to the accompaniment of a severe tongue-lashing from "Mum" for our apparent apathy and uncaring attitude. Taking our leave, we retreated to the camping area to resurrect the fallen tents and to retrieve various scattered belongings, before re-assembling back at the taverna to continue with the evening's proceedings.

Two days later we left for the Yugoslav border and the drive back through Europe. On our return to England, despite the "hiccup" in Heraclizia, Rachel had appeared to enjoy her Greek trip; she seemed a happier person, who was more able to cope with life's little upsets. I spent several days in London with Hannah before leaving on the next trip to Turkey, which would take me through to late October and the end of the season.

1971 Frontier brochure

Travelling back from Turkey I pulled into Heraclizia for the last time that year and parked the minibus on the headland camping area. As I wandered down to George's Taverna on the beach, I could hear "It's All Over Now" by the Rolling Stones playing on the jukebox. There was a solitary figure with a bottle of ouzo sitting at a table next to a pole that supported the thatched canopy; they were banging their head against the post in time to the music. As I moved closer, I realized it was Stu Sissons, although his head, which normally sported a fine crop of hair, was shaved - and he was in bad shape. I sat down, called to George to turn the jukebox down and managed to get Stu's attention. Recognizing me, he started crying, eventually telling me that he'd arrived in Heraclizia from Turkey the previous day. I ordered some food and as we ate, Stu's story unfolded.

A couple of weeks earlier, he had checked in to Camping Londra in Istanbul with a group; that evening, around midnight, he had been skinny dipping with a couple of the women from the trip. Maybe someone had made a complaint as, out of the blue, a couple of policemen arrived in a squad car, took in the scene and told Stu to leave. Stu, having a pretty good idea of what might happen to two naked girls left alone with these two men, ran back to his minibus and grabbed an axe that he kept under the driver's seat "for protection". Then he ran back to the pool waving the axe and yelling at the coppers, telling them (basically) to leave. Five minutes later about half a dozen squad cars arrived and Stu was arrested at gunpoint, taken to the local police station and charged with threatening police officers with a dangerous weapon. The next morning, he was taken to the notorious Sağmalcılar prison (which featured in the film *"Midnight Express"*), where he was to be held on remand until his trial; his head was shaved, in common with the other prisoners.

The British Consul eventually contacted his father and explained that, if it went to trial Stu was facing a sentence of 25 years under Turkish law. To avoid this, he needed to provide bail money of £1,000. They could then issue Stu with a new passport under an assumed name in order to get him out of the country (the police having confiscated Stu's passport on his arrest). Stu's father flew to Istanbul the next day and paid the bail. A new passport was issued and Stu crossed the border into northern Greece the following day, as Stuart Healey. He had been incarcerated in Sağmalcılar for just two weeks, but had clearly been a traumatic experience, as it had temporatily turned him into a nervous wreck. Happily, the next time I saw him he had fully recovered and was back to his old self.

It had been a fascinating summer and a steep learning curve, but the acquaintances and friends I had made would stand me in good stead in the future.

7. WINTER '71

During the summer, Frontier had filmed a promotional video in Morocco and that Autumn and throughout the winter they arranged showings a couple of evenings a week at the Nomad Travellers' Club situated at Sussex Gardens in London – a popular meeting place and watering hole for Aussies, Kiwis and South Africans. It was arranged for three or four drivers to attend each showing, frequent the bar area, mix with the clientele and take bookings for the following year. One of the drivers, Matt Davies, had attended drama school before running a wine bar in Knightsbridge and then joining Frontier. He loved hamming it up with a limp-wristed gay act, resulting in some nervous looks from our generally macho colonial friends and muttered comments about "a bloody poofter"! As the evening went on, Matt would become more and more outrageous, until we burst out laughing and everyone realized it was all an act. There was a great camaraderie between the drivers at these sessions and, needless to say we had some very enjoyable evenings - and we even managed to rustle up some business!

While I had been driving around Greece and Turkey in the latter part of the season, Gus and Micky Hines had been chosen to take Frontier's first ever overland trip to India and Nepal driving two Land Rovers. Apparently, it had been a really tough trip and, on their return, one that they had both vowed never to do again.

I had been in constant touch with Hannah, who was working as a receptionist at a hotel in Munich. The hotel was closing for Christmas and, as she was the only member of staff who was staying in residence, she suggested that I might want to join her for the festive period. It was to be the first Christmas I had ever spent away from home and my family. I travelled to Munich by train, sitting for most of the journey opposite a little old lady dressed in peasant clothes whose world-weary eyes seemed to bear the sorrow of 1,000 goodbyes.

After a wonderful, snow-bound Munich Christmas with Hannah I returned to England and found an invitation to a New Year's Eve party from the Frontier photographers Ted and Caroline. It was being organized by Caroline's sister. Gus and I drove from Brighton to the venue, a large country mansion outside Chelmsford, stopping off in Brentwood to pick up my younger sister Liz. The guests consisted of a strange mix of society "trendies" and Frontier people including a few hand-picked drivers, myself and Gus included. I was delighted to find Roy from Heraclizia also in attendance! During the course of the evening, I was approached by Colin Payten and asked if I would like to take the next India trip leaving at the end of February, which would be the first attempt at completing the return trip in a Transit. I thought for a moment, but decided I could not refuse if I wanted to further my career with the company, so accepted the offer. Then I began to recall what Gus and Micky, two experienced drivers, using Land Rovers, had said about the trip and it suddenly dawned on me just what I had agreed to do; it's one thing to spend a summer driving around

Europe and North Africa, but quite another to take a Transit on the 21,000 mile round trip to Calcutta via Nepal and back in the scheduled time of 14 weeks!

It was a night of drunken revelry for the overland contingent, while the trendy set were a little more sedate. At one stage I saw Gus disappearing outside with Liz. I knew all about Gus Fraser's reputation with women and was also aware that there were a few Transit minibuses parked in the driveway that lent themselves quite well to the gentle art of seduction, as most overland drivers had discovered. I immediately jumped to the conclusion that my sister needed rescuing. Picking up a handy golf club from the umbrella rack beside the door, I set off in hot pursuit, racing up and down the row of Transits and peering in through the windows, not realizing that I was being watched by Gus and Liz as they stood in the porch doubled up in silent laughter. They had apparently wandered outside to get some fresh air. I retreated back inside, red-faced and mumbling under my breath about shady overland characters disappearing with 18-year-old "innocents". Whenever Gus wanted to wind me up over the next few years he would state, with a mischievous twinkle in his eye, that he would marry my sister one day and then we would be "family". And he did eventually! But that's another story.

I returned with Gus to Brighton to prepare for my India trip and the two of us took up residence at 5 Granville Road, Gus commandeering a spare bed, as Dimitris was now living and studying in London, while I had the sofa and my trusty sleeping bag. We started working part-time for Dave Latchford, a friend of Gus's who ran a fleet of self-drive vans and minibuses, making enough money to pay our way at the flat by driving and servicing the vehicles. I was writing to Hannah in Munich virtually on a daily basis until, horror of horrors, the Post Office workers came out on strike. I was devastated! After a few days, the phone bill at the flat began to rise quite rapidly as I tried to persuade Hannah to leave her job at the hotel and join me on the India trip, but to no avail, as her Teutonic pragmatism told her that it would not be a sensible choice. I was heartbroken – but India beckoned.

8. İNDİA

EUROPE

At seven o'clock one morning towards the end of February 1971, I set out for India. Everyone was still asleep as I was leaving the flat in Granville Road, when I suddenly realised that I didn't actually possess a warm jacket to combat the winter weather I'd encounter while travelling across Europe and western Asia. Gus's top-of-the-range windcheater hung invitingly on the back of the door and, rather than wake him, I decided to help myself – after all, I had made a down-payment on it in Belgian francs in Zeebrugge a year earlier! I drove to Crawley to collect Stewart Yates, the co-driver I had arranged to take on for the trip. Stu was an unassuming person with a wickedly dry sense of humour, who had asked if I could persuade Colin to let him join me on the trip as a co-driver.

As this was, by all accounts, going to be a particularly difficult journey judging by Gus and Micky's reactions on their return in December, I had prepared myself both mentally and physically for it. Gus and Micky were both experienced drivers and had been driving Land Rovers, while I was a comparative beginner and was to be undertaking the trip in a Transit. I came to the conclusion that a co-driver would be a useful addition to the trip and had managed to convince Colin that it would be a good move. Stu was delighted when I broke the news to him; he was going to India - but as an unpaid courier! I had been preparing the vehicle and trying to organise equipment for the journey over the previous month. However, thanks to our Operations Manager, Pat Russell, and his tight purse strings, I was still short of several items I had requested as we left Crawley, including snow-chains and folding shovels.

As usual, we rendezvoused with our passengers at Victoria Coach Station. They included Anna - an 18 year-old Australian, Peter – a steward with British Rail, John – an Englishman who was an officer in the New Zealand merchant navy, his wife Jill, Guntaj – a Sikh student who was returning home to India plus a young French lady by the name of Michelle. Guntaj was going as far as Kabul and would then have to fly from there to India, as Pakistan and India were on a war footing, Peter and Michelle were embarking on the round trip, while the remainder were going to Calcutta and then travelling on from there back to Australia and New Zealand.

After an initial briefing on what to expect during the journey, we set off for Dover, caught the ferry and drove through to Frankfurt. The temperature that night was decidedly cool for camping at -7C! The next night saw us in Munich where I arranged a rendezvous with Hannah in a last-ditch effort to persuade her to join me on the trip, sadly to no avail. I never saw or heard from her again. From Munich we progressed through Austria and Yugoslavia and on into Greece. The itinerary took in Athens, stopping at Meteora on the way. There was snow lying at the side of the road as we made our way up to the monasteries that morning. As we drove back around midday the snow was melting in the warm sunshine, revealing the first Spring flowers that had been buried beneath their winter blanket, their bright colours sparkling, as small rivulets of melt-water ran between the rocks. It truly felt like Spring had arrived.

We spent a couple of days in Athens before heading up to Heraclizia where the villagers were amazed to see us this early in the year. Needless to say, they made us very welcome and we spent a relaxing day there before moving on to Istanbul, where Mustapha was also pleasantly surprised at such an early start to his season. As ever, we were looked after extremely well and everyone enjoyed the superb cuisine and sights of this bustling historic city where East meets West.

Occasionally a passenger would experience stomach upsets while on a trip; I once had a passenger who, after spending his first night out of England on a campsite in Cologne, announced that he was suffering from European tummy! However, our BR steward Peter had the opposite problem and despite indulging in the culinary delights on the way down through Europe, had been unable to evacuate his bowels for two weeks - to everyone's increasing concern. After ten days we had come to the conclusion that he must be creating some sort of record worthy of the Guinness Book of Records. However, Istanbul bought an end to this mammoth bout of constipation much to everyone's, and particularly Peter's, relief. Although, disappointingly for some, it was apparently not the spectacular event we had all been expecting; just a fairly normal "download" by all accounts!

TURKEY

Europe was left in the wake of the Bosporus ferry as we crossed to Asia and camped overnight outside the town of Bilecek. The following morning, we were engulfed in a blizzard as we drove through the mountains heading south and I found myself driving virtually blind on roads of variable quality. Dropping down from the mountains to the coast we were transported from mid-winter to spring in the space of some 30 miles. We camped in an orange grove outside Alanya and I spent the next day giving the Transit a general service while the passengers gave her a much-needed wash. That afternoon we drove up to a small mountain village set on a forested plateau, with a beautiful view of the Taurus Mountains in one direction and out across the Aegean in another.

On leaving Alanya we took a winding clifftop route along the coast to Mersin, passing through orange and lemon groves and banana plantations – some of the most beautiful scenery I had seen in Turkey. At Mersin we met some Germans who had just returned from India. They told me that the northern route out of Tehran was closed and that there had been heavy snowfalls in Kabul; I just hoped that conditions would have improved by the time we got there. Apparently, the road we had taken through the mountains from Afyon to Alanya was now blocked by snow, so we had just made it in time. Before leaving Mersin, I had a blowing exhaust welded and recharged our gas bottles. We took a twisty mountainous route inland to Pozanti and on to Nigde before arriving at Nevsehir and the incredible Goreme Valley. The whole area resembled a moonscape, with huge conical rock formations carved from volcanic deposits over aeons by wind and rain. Early Cappadocians carved homes from the rock.

Later, when Christianity arrived in the area, they also carved out churches, creating an elaborate underground city. There were beautiful centuries-old frescoes in several of the churches, while the strange landscape with its troglodyte dwellings was a wonder to behold. It was cold after the warmth of the coast, with a dusting of snow on the ground, so we took a chalet at the Paris Motel and squeezed the whole group into one room with their sleeping bags arranged side-by-side across the floor.

The drive from Goreme to Sivas was depressing; the road took us across a flat, featureless plain, deteriorating badly after Gemerek and as we moved into central and eastern Turkey the country and people seemed to regress to the early twentieth century. It was a dismal, cold and windy day and we encountered several dust storms before arriving on the outskirts of Sivas. The "campsite" shown as a BP Mocamp on the tourist map turned out to be a semi-frozen, hard and bumpy ploughed field beside a two-pump petrol station with very limited facilities. It was one o'clock in the afternoon and had started to rain. Stu and I had a discussion about the options open to us and decided that, provided the passengers were agreeable, we should carry on driving that afternoon and through the night, with Stu and I taking it in turns to sleep on the triple seat behind the front seats. The extra day we made up could potentially be spent in Tehran. Needless to say, faced with the prospect of erecting tents and spending the night on a frozen ploughed field, everyone agreed to carry on. After a brew-up we set off again at about three o'clock, stopping briefly in Sivas before continuing.

I was still doing all the driving, as Stu didn't fancy the conditions - and I couldn't blame him. About two miles out of town, driving towards the mountains, we came to a road block manned by half a dozen soldiers. As the bus drew to a halt, an officer approached.

"I am sorry, you have to turn back – there is too much snow in the mountains and it is very dangerous to travel tonight."

"It's OK", I assured him, "We're English", (as if that would somehow negate any potential danger that lay ahead). "We'll just go and look", I added in a re-assuring voice.

The officer shrugged. "You have snow chains?"

"No, we don't need them – see double rear wheels!" I delivered this statement with the utmost bravado.

The officer glanced at one of his men and raised his eyebrows. Then he looked back at me, shrugged his shoulders and made a dismissive gesture with his hand. "O.K., you go".

He was right – there was a lot of snow! It was heavy going climbing up into the mountains on an atrocious road and the situation rapidly deteriorated as we were engulfed in a heavy blizzard. It was dark by now and we were the only vehicle on the road. I was becoming mesmerised by the driving snow and my mind began to play tricks on me. I kept thinking that the bus was stationary; that it wasn't actually moving at all; that it was just the snow that was conjuring up the illusion of movement. I shook my head to clear my mind, took a cigarette from the pack on the dash board and lit it, hoping the process of smoking would help me concentrate. I stopped the bus several times during the night, getting out, running round the vehicle two or three times and rubbing my face with snow to clear my head.

I was now driving on packed virgin snow and we got bogged down twice, but with everyone out and pushing we eventually reached the town of Susehri. We really could have done with shovels on that stage of the journey and I was cursing Pat Russell and his tight purse strings. The weather changed dramatically with the altitude and a descent of a couple of hundred feet or so was enough to turn the heavy snow into rain. The road was now virtually all un-surfaced and unstable, as we carried on, encountering heavy snow again between Refahiye and Erzincan. At 11.45pm we took a 15 minute toilet stop. Compared to the conditions we had already experienced, the going wasn't too bad, although I had a bit of a hair-raising experience as we dropped down out of the mountains towards Erzurum at about 3.30am. I was driving down a steep incline and feeling a bit drowsy, when I suddenly realised there was a sharp switch-back at the bottom of the slope with a sheer drop on the far side. I was approaching the bend too fast for comfort, but it would have been suicidal to touch the brakes on packed snow. With my heart in my mouth, I managed to slide the Transit round the bend while the passengers and Stu slept on, unaware of how close we had come to disaster - and the resulting headlines in the UK press.

We passed through Erzurum at 4.00am, heading for Agri and the Iranian border. Two hours later the front axle, which was low-slung on a Transit, became bogged down in a snowdrift on a pass between Horasan and Tahir, but we eventually managed to dig ourselves out using the tin plates from our "traveller's kitchen". Once again, I cursed Pat Russell - he was not flavour of the month!

*Driving through the mountains in
Eastern Turkey - March'71*

*Bogged down in a snowdrift in
Eastern Turkey - March '71*

We could see snow ploughs making their way down the mountain-side, so we decided to turn back to Horasan and wait for them to clear the road. We found an early-morning tea shop and sat round the ancient wood-burning stove in the centre of the room, sipping our glasses of black tea and enjoying the warmth. Several heavy trans-continental lorries that had been stuck in the town were now moving, so at 7.45 we tried again. As we climbed up the pass, the lorries were queueing at the side of the road and putting on snow chains. It was slow going at 10 to 15 miles an hour, with constant delays as a lorry would get stuck and have to wait for another to pull it free. Further up the pass we met an English lorry driver who had managed just 20 miles in the previous 24 hours. However, the Transit (with its double rear wheels) just kept on going with little or no trouble, passing through Agri at 11.45am and eventually arriving at the Iranian border, having passed Mount Ararat on the way, at 2.15pm.

İRAN

The clocks went forward one-and-a-half hours at the border, making it 3.45pm local time. The Iranian customs officers were not the most co-operative that I had encountered, to say the least, but we eventually completed the border formalities and were allowed to leave at 6.20pm. The road to Tabriz was excellent and we arrived at 9.30pm local time. I had driven 945 miles in 36 hours through very challenging conditions, with just a couple of short breaks since leaving Goreme the previous morning. I was both physically and mentally exhausted. I have often looked back at that drive and wondered why I did it. I suppose the simple answer is that it seemed like a good idea at the time! We found the campsite closed, as it had not yet opened for the new summer season, but shortly after we arrived the manager appeared, unlocked the gates for us and conducted as to permanently erected tents on concrete bases, complete with beds and mattresses. I collapsed into bed to wake early next morning feeling surprisingly refreshed.

It was a 400-mile drive to Tehran, a straight run on good, desert roads. Despite the roads being busy due to the start of the Muslim New Year, we made it in ten hours and set up camp at Camping Gol-E-Sahra on the far side of the city. Tehran is probably the worst place that I've ever driven in. It was similar to Istanbul in that there seemed to be no rules - or if there were, no one bothered with them. Nobody gave way and traffic lights tended to be ignored after dark. The only difference in Tehran was that the traffic was twice as fast as Istanbul and every single taxi, even the new ones, had at least one dent or body repair. It was definitely a case of the survival of the fittest.

We had picked the wrong time to arrive in Tehran, as everything of interest, including the Peacock Throne and the Crown Jewels were closed, so we amused ourselves by wandering through the bazaar and main shopping centre, which were both open. In Ferdowsi Avenue opposite the British Embassy, there was a shop where you could buy any currency you wished, including Russian and Chinese, at very favourable black-market rates. Our evenings were spent at the bowling alley and entertainments centre in Kourosh-E- Kabir Avenue, one of the few places that sold beer.

The extra day we had made up by driving overnight through Eastern Turkey was spent servicing the Transit, while the passengers busied themselves cleaning the camping equipment.

Anna, our Australian, had not been able to get an Afghan visa before leaving the UK, so the next morning we collected her visa from the Afghan embassy, did some shopping and left Tehran around mid-day, heading for Meshad. This was the last stop on our journey where we would be able to find campsites; after that, we would be using small, inexpensive hotels. We took the southern route to Sari which is on the Caspian Sea, as the main route through the mountains was heavily snowed up and icy. The road was awful and the going was slow on the unmetalled surface, but the scenery was spectacular as barren mountains changed to lush, fertile valleys. The Caspian seemed to create a micro-climate for the surrounding area and the trees were full of Spring blossom. We were back on a properly-surfaced road and carried on through Gorgan to Shah-Passand. Arriving at 11.45pm, we stopped for a quick meal. There appeared to be a shortage of eating houses in Iran, and the few that were available had very limited menus, the standard offering being shashlik kebab – a mutton kebab served with boiled rice and a raw egg. The idea was that you broke the egg, mixed it into the rice, and the heat of the rice cooked the egg as you stirred it – presuming that the rice was warm enough!

We left an hour later, having decided to drive through the night and push on to Mashad. The road deteriorated badly after Shah-Passand; the constant pounding had caused the exhaust to fracture, making the Transit sound like a turbo-charged tractor and causing people to run for cover in every town we passed through. There were some alarming pot holes on the road and very few filling stations, but we eventually reached Meshad at 10.30 the following morning, only to find the city full of pilgrims. Meshad is the holy city of Iran attracting 20 million tourists and pilgrims a year; in the previous few days the population had swollen from 700,000 to 2,000,000. The campsites were full, so we drove around for some time looking for a hotel with room for us, but to no avail. Finally, we were flagged down by an English-speaking student who introduced himself as Valee. He explained that at times like this, when large numbers of pilgrims were visiting and all the hotels, hostels and campsites were full, all the schools were opened up and people allowed to stay in the school buildings. We had to obtain a letter of recommendation from the Tourist Office to the janitor of a local school (who happened to be Valee's uncle), which then entitled us to free board and lodging. Arriving at the school, we found what I can only describe as a modern-day kavanseri. All the school furniture had been cleared to the sides of the very large classrooms and the floors covered with an assortment of rugs (Persian, of course), with family groups staking claim to an area, where they were cooking, eating and sleeping. We quickly staked our claim and proceeded to set up camp. Needless to say, this band of infidels amongst a room-full of Muslim pilgrims was the object of much curiosity and animated conversation.

I gave the Transit a thorough service the next day, while the group had a conducted tour of the city with Valee. As well as the broken exhaust, one of the inner rear tyres was punctured and the plug from the top of the gearbox was missing, together with most of the oil. I managed to get everything fixed and we left Meshad at 8.30 the following morning. My lasting memory of the city is the awful smell of boiled mutton that permeated the city centre. In the way that we have our fish-and-chip shops in the UK, so Iranis have shops that sell boiled sheep heads. When cooked, the heads were piled in the shop window; it was a most un-nerving experience when you first happened on one of these establishments to find all these skulls staring out at you.

When they were sold, the heads were split open and the brains were consumed, presumably with great relish!

AFGHANİSTAN

We arrived at the Afghan border early in the afternoon and the clocks went forward another hour. My first impression of Afghanistan was of a very poor country that was struggling to survive. The border guards were dressed in what appeared to be another army's patched-up cast-offs, with most of them wearing sandals rather than army boots, as they gathered round the mini-bus asking us for food. We needed Afghan currency for some petrol and the compulsory road tax costing 650 Afghani, but there was no official money exchange bureau and we got a significantly lower rate than the official 300 Afghani to the pound from the army officer in charge of the border post - presumably, this was one of his perks. It was a short drive of 70 miles to Herat; after arriving late in the afternoon we took rooms at the Hotel Super Behzad at 30Afs per room. The meal of chicken, rice and vegetables that evening cost a similar amount and was very tasty and most welcome after the bland monotony of the Iranian fare. We spent the following day in the city visiting the local market and generally sight-seeing.

Leaving Herat, we drove south-east to Kandahar on the main highway that takes you from one side of the country to the other. The road was extremely good, the section from Herat to Kandahar having been built by the Russians, while the section from Kandahar to Kabul and onward through the Kabul Gorge to Jalalabad was built by the Americans. There were only a few filling stations en route and, although petrol was very cheap at

6Afs for a litre, Gus had warned me that the pump attendants were very sharp and needed to be watched like a hawk. During his trip with Micky, he had become so incensed with the constant cheating that, on one occasion, he had grabbed the pump nozzle from the attendant, stuffed it in his mouth and started to fill him up with "super". He was subsequently chased from the petrol station by knife-wielding tribesmen! To avoid any "misunderstandings" I would ask for a set amount of fuel and tender the exact amount of money. However, it didn't stop one crafty operator from getting the better of me. I had asked for 50 litres of fuel and gave him 300Afs before turning round to replace the fuel cap, but when I turned back, he confronted me with two 100 notes plus one 10Af note, which was a very similar colour to the 100, but smaller. There was no way I would have mistaken the two; he'd obviously switched one of the 100s for a 10, but I couldn't argue with him and reluctantly had to cough up another 90Afs.

There were toll posts about every 100km along the road to Kandahar, the charge being 10 or 15Afs at each stop. The landscape was barren desert with a few isolated villages; we arrived mid-afternoon, booking in at the Pamir Hotel. Afghan hotels at 25 to 30 Afs a night provided you with a bed with clean sheets and at least one shower somewhere on the premises. Hot water was provided by a wood-burning boiler and you could always tell when the water was warming up, as you the smell of burning wood drifted through the corridors in the morning. Kandahar reminded me a little of Morocco, with the market full of carpets, brightly coloured Afghan shirts and hustlers trying to sell you the local hashish at $8 a kilo.

Afghanistan - March '71

Afghanistan was part of the ancient East/West trading route and the people, who had been used to strangers travelling through their country over the centuries, were indifferent to our presence while still acknowledging us. They were some of the best people I encountered in Asia, being genuinely polite and friendly. I always felt at ease there and came to regard the country as the Asian equivalent of Greece - minus the beaches. We left Kandahar early next morning to drive the 320 miles to Kabul via Ghazni. The journey was a lot more interesting than the previous day, with views of distant mountains. As we passed through a number of villages, we saw what I at first thought were forts, but later discovered were karavansari – traditional resting places where travellers, over the centuries, could stop and where, by tradition, no harm would befall them.

Kabul, on first impressions, was impressive, with the Hindu Kush rising behind the city and glowing golden-red in the evening sunlight. There were plenty of small hotels scattered around the city catering for the many young travellers on the "hippy trail"; we took rooms at the Green Hotel situated on Chicken Street, so called because there was a market at one end where – you guessed it - live chickens were bought and sold. Although appearing scruffy and under-developed, Kabul was a fascinating place where you could buy virtually anything at a fraction of the European price, including English and American cigarettes. Around the corner from Chicken Street was a market where you could find all sorts of "luxuries" such as Kellogg's cornflakes, Cadbury's chocolate and Swiss cheese, although none of these were cheap. You could find great lumps of locally-mined lapis lazuli and semi-precious stones that could be bought for next to nothing, as well as beautifully made Afghan coats, jackets made from wolf skins and calf-length boots made to measure from camel hide. The place was a mecca for the European and American kids on their way to India and Kathmandu. In an enclosed square was an unofficial money market with currency shops, all seemingly run by Sikhs, situated on two tiers around the square, where you were able to buy virtually any currency including Pakistani rupees at 25 and Indian rupees at 29 to the pound. The official rate was 11.5 and 18.5 respectively and neither currency was supposed to be purchased outside of those countries, so the money had to be well hidden.

The next morning, we were all afflicted with "Kabul tummy" – a type of dysentery peculiar to Kabul that lasted for 24 hours. It was one of the quirks of the city and despite being very careful about what I ate and drank, I subsequently succumbed to this on the first day of every visit I made to Kabul, which was the only place I regularly suffered from an upset stomach. However, we proceeded to discover some excellent eating places including the Marco Polo which served the very best Afghan food and the 25 Hours Club with its Chinese cuisine.

The 25 Hour Club was owned by Ali Shiraz, who quickly became a firm friend. His Grandfather, Muhammad Nadir Shah, had been the Shah of Afghanistan in the 1920s and Ali told me how he had been overthrown by a British-instigated uprising by several hill tribes and eventually assassinated in 1933. His son and Ali's uncle, Muhammad Zahir Shah, had succeeded him and remained on the throne until he, himself, was eventually deposed in 1973. Ali explained how his grandfather had been a progressive monarch who made the mistake of many similar Muslim rulers - building schools instead of mosques. He was also the first leader to allow his wife to appear in public out of purdah, which incensed the clergy, who stirred up trouble among the people. According to Ali, the British, who had always wanted to gain a foothold in the country, decided to capitalise on this by superimposing a photo of the queen's face onto that of a nude body. Then, aided by Muhammad Zahir Shah, they had recruited a local bandit to roam the Hindu Kush and circulate the photo around the hill tribes, who then rose up and marched on Kabul. However, when Ali's uncle came to the throne, the British were promptly thrown out of the country. Ali had been educated in Paris and the USA, owned the only Jaguar in Afghanistan at the time (an old Mk 10), ran the only estate agents as well as the 25 Hour club and was probably the first and only playboy in the country at that time!

Before continuing our journey, we said goodbye to our Sikh companion Guntaj, who arranged to rendezvous with us when we reached Delhi, and drove up through the stunning scenery of the Kabul Gorge with its rugged mountains, tumbling rivers and serene, azure blue lakes. The road snaked between sheer cliff faces, through dark mountain tunnels and on through to the provincial capital of Jalalabad before reaching the Pakistan border at the top of the Khyber Pass. Sitting at the head of the Khyber was the town of Landi Kotal, where the local cottage industry was the manufacture of working replicas of any firearm you cared to name. The town was also notorious as a drugs-clearing point. Drugs and life were cheap; hashish (Afghan cannabis resin), was $8 a kilo and a pint of blood could be sold to hospitals for $6. Word had it that it wasn't uncommon for a dumped body to be found completely drained of blood. A lot of young travellers were falling victim to "bad acid", and I had met several elderly people while in Kabul who were searching for sons and daughters who had gone missing in this region.

PAKISTAN

The Afghan customs was predictably shambolic, while the Pakistanis were a model of bureaucratic efficiency, with neat shelves full of bulging files that looked as though they might well go back to the year dot. There was a tax of 11 rupees to pay for passage through the Khyber; this went directly to the

Pashtun hill tribes to ensure the safe passage of travellers through the pass. However, the road was closed at dusk to avoid the possibility of attack and robbery after dark, which by all accounts would be a distinct possibility. The road was rough and slightly disappointing after the splendour of the Kabul Gorge, but the pass held an air of menace; as we passed the Fort of the Khyber Rifles it conjured up visions of the soldiers of the British Raj fighting off attacks from fierce local tribesmen.

Arriving in Peshawar late that afternoon we took rooms at the local Dak bungalows which provided cheap, but rough accommodation for travellers. Pakistan was a frantic experience after the calm of Afghanistan, the streets of Peshawar being a turmoil of brightly-painted lorries, noisy motor bikes, over-laden donkeys and skinny, sad-looking horses. On the bustling streets you could buy anything from diamonds and gold, or a home-made Kalashnikov, to silks from Swat in the North-West Frontier Province and deliciously-spiced street food.

Our onward journey took us through crowded towns and villages to Rawalpindi and Islamabad. Then we drove on to Lahore, where we booked into the centrally-located Parkway Hotel. We rose early the next morning to obtain border passes (Pakistan and India were sabre rattling at the time). These came from the Home Office located in the Mall which took a long time to locate, as the local pronunciation is "Moll" and I was chastised for not pronouncing the word properly! The process was very efficient, taking about an hour – and we even had tea and cake served to us! Afterwards, we went to relax in a local park, but were surrounded by crowds of people who gathered like flies to a sticky bun. We ended up at a coffee house in the Mall and had a fascinating discussion with a politically-minded man who was very informative and invited us to his house where we spent a good evening chatting and enjoying beers, whisky and gin with him and some of his friends.

The next day proved to be the start of a very trying 48 hours. We arrived at the border late in the morning, and passed through the Pakistani customs only to find on our imminent entry to India, that Michelle (the most awkward and miserable person on the trip) didn't have the required visa for a French citizen to enter the country. I couldn't just abandon her there, so I turned back to the Pakistani customs which we were able to navigate without difficulty thanks to a police chief who required a lift to Lahore, the barriers being raised in double-quick time. To obtain a visa for Michelle we had to travel back to Islamabad – a journey of some 200 miles. We also had to get new border passes for the group, but found the office in Lahore closed. We arrived in Islamabad at 9.30pm, and found the Indian High Commission on Embassy Road. However, as this was an administrative centre consisting of embassies, high commissions and government offices, there were no hotels in the area, so we slept the night in, on and around the minibus.

Michelle and I were on the doorstep when the Commission opened at 8.00 the next morning, but were told the visa would not be ready until 12.30, so we went off to try and locate the local Home Office. We were directed to Rawalpindi and then back to Islamabad, just managing to get all the required documents before everything closed at 2.00pm. At 6.30, we finally arrived back in Lahore, where we had to spend another night, as the border at Ferozpur closed at sunset.

İNDİA

So, if you fail, try again! We drove back to the border where the formalities took about two hours, including a half-hearted search of our pockets by the Indian customs officers looking for rupees and drugs. The clocks went forward half an hour and then we had a long, hard day travelling through to Delhi, constantly avoiding bullocks, carts, cyclists and crazy pedestrians, none of which appeared to have any road sense. We finally arrived in the early evening and booked into the Vishwa Yuvak Kendra International Youth Centre, which provided good modern comfortable accommodation.

Delhi was the beginning of the "India experience", a sudden awakening to a vibrancy of life and a riot of sound and colour, but also to the huge contrast between the extreme wealth of people with gold, fine clothes and beautiful jewellery dripping from them and the abject poverty of beggars asking for baksheesh. At the centre of New Delhi was Connaught Place, a gyratory consisting of three concentric circles with the inner circle housing the aptly named Central Park where the country's first Wimpy Hamburger Bar had been established. The inner circle was fringed with colonnaded Georgian-style buildings and traders had set up book stalls under the colonnades, with a lot of literature on Hinduism, Buddhism, astrology and palm reading, as well as modern and classic works of fiction. Meanwhile, the United Coffee House, a relic of the British Raj, proved to be the ideal place to take refuge from the oppressive heat and humidity and hustle and bustle of the street. The air-conditioning was so strong, that, after a few minutes, I would begin to shiver. Then, when I left through the double doors it was as though I had walked into an oven. The highlight of our stay in

Delhi was meeting up again with our Sikh friend Guntaj who, together with his father, took the group to the famous Natraj restaurant close to the Red Fort in Old Delhi, renowned for its tandoori dishes. Guntaj insisted on me trying his favourite dish of Matar Paneer (cheese and peas curry) which was absolutely delicious and, which has become one of my all-time favourites. Before we left, Guntaj invited us to stay with him and his family towards the end of our trip, as his father was chief of mining in a coal-mining town about 70 miles from Calcutta.

***

Leaving Delhi we made the relatively short drive to Agra and the Taj Mahal. The Taj was stunning – a perfection of white marble. It was commissioned by Shah Jahan in 1631, to be built in the memory of his wife Mumtaz Mahal, who died on 17 June that year, while giving birth to their 14th child. Construction started in 1632, and the mausoleum was completed in 1648. Built on the banks of the Yamuna River, with a backdrop of an azure-blue sky, it was and is still the one building that lived up to, and exceeded, all my expectations. I went back at dusk and watched a colony of flying foxes wing its way across the front of the mausoleum as the moon rose – it was magical.

The following day we were thrilled to see bands of monkeys, flocks of parrots and strutting peacocks as we travelled along quiet country roads to Khajuraho, a small peaceful village that was beginning to gain popularity as a tourist destination due to a cluster of ancient Jain temples that had been rediscovered by a British surveyor, T.S. Burt, back in the 1830s. We found our way to Jain Lodge, a small family house belonging to Mr and Mrs

Jain and their 5 children. Two rooms were made available for the group with mattresses placed on the floor while I bartered with Mrs Jain over the price of a meal for us that evening. Jains are strict vegetarians and the thali meal comprising of about 10 different dishes accompanied by potato pancakes served to us by the children was superb. It is still one of the best Indian meals I've ever had – all at the princely sum of 2.5 rupees (12.5p) a head!

The temples at Khajuraho were amazing, built between the 10th and 13th centuries during the rule of the Chandela dynasty, worshippers of Vishnu and Shiva, and covered top-to-bottom, inside and out with intricately carved statues, including numerous erotic carvings that depict men, women, and even animals engaged in lovemaking and orgies under the benign smiles of divine beings. It was all a bit of an eye-opener!

Our next stop was Benares (now Varanasi), known as the eternal city or the city of the dead. It is situated on the banks of the Ganges and is the holiest of the seven sacred cities in Hinduism and Jainism. The city was a heaving throng of pilgrims, as Hindus believe that dying here and getting cremated along the banks of the sacred river Ganges allows them to break the cycle of rebirth and attain liberation. We booked into the Mint Hotel. Owned by the Maharajah of Benares and built some 200 years ago, it had been used in bygone years as a mint and later as a hospital. It had large, cool rooms with high ceilings. The manager, who was also the Maharaja's financial adviser, provided us with a guide, Luke - a student who was an Indian Christian. Over the next three days Luke took us into the centre of the city, through its narrow, chaotic streets packed with people visiting the multitude of religious shrines and offering up flowers to their chosen deity, to visit the silk weavers in the Muslim quarter. He also took us to Sarnath, about 10km outside Benares, where Buddha gave his famous first sermon, preaching his message of the middle way to nirvana.

At the crack of dawn on the second morning Luke took us down to the Ganges to board a boat for a trip to view the famous Ghats, the ancient steps leading down to the river where people washed clothes, bathed and prayed, and the many temples and shrines along its banks. On our way I mentioned that I had a pair of treasured buffalo-hide sandals with a broken toe loop that needed mending. We stopped on a street corner where a man, the local cobbler, sat on the pavement with an old orange box holding his needles, thread, polish, brushes, etc. Having left the sandals with him to repair, we went back that evening to collect them and there he was, still sitting there with his orange box – and my re-furbished sandals. The cost was 25 paise (just over 1p). I fished in my pocket and pulled out a 50 paise coin. The cobbler started looking for change and I told him it was OK – he could keep it. As we got back into the minibus Luke turned to me and asked, angrily, why I had given him "all that money". I pointed out that it was only 50 paise, but according to Luke I was already being overcharged and the money I had given him was what he would normally earn in a whole day; consequently, as he had made his money for the next day, he wouldn't be there when people turned up the next day to get their shoes mended. Apparently, I had disrupted the entire system by giving this man the equivalent of 2.5p!

On our last day, the hotel manager, recognizing a possible source of future income from visiting groups, invited Stu and me for a tour of the old, and now redundant, Maharaja's palace. It was something of a surreal experience for me, a lad from an Essex council estate, being shown round the palace where the Queen and Prince Philip had stayed during their tour of India ten years earlier. We were ushered, with great reverence, into the bedroom where the royal couple had slept. Finally, at the end of our conducted tour, we were offered some whisky served by a man in a white uniform - which our host hoped was OK, as it was 25 years old!

Leaving Benares we headed off on a two day drive to Nepal and Kathmandu, travelling past Patna and into Bihar, probably the poorest state in India. Stopping off the first night in Muzaffarpur, we checked into the Lions Club, a sad, run-down relic of the British Raj that sported a threadbare billiards table and elderly stewards dressed in tatty "white" tunics and turbans. Being a regular famine area at that time, there was no food available so we were advised to head for the railway station where we eventually tracked down a little stall selling chana masala and rice. We left early the next morning along the narrow, crowded road to the Nepalese border at Berganj.

NEPAL

The road from the border to Kathmandu was simply stunning. The first 30 miles were a good flat stretch built by the Chinese, which was transformed dramatically transformed into a narrow, twisty and bumpy road as we began to climb up into the foothills of the Himalayas, with lush, secluded valleys rich in vegetation and glimpses of the most magnificent, snow-covered mountains imaginable reaching up to touch the sky. It was a difficult road to negotiate, with the occasional bus or lorry coming in the opposite direction and little room to make a passing manoeuvre, but was nevertheless one of the most beautiful and memorable roads I ever traversed. Eighteen months earlier, I had been a parochial Essex lad setting out on my first trip abroad - and here I was now, in Nepal, having travelled half way round the world through Europe, Asia and the Indian subcontinent, on the roof of the world surrounded by the towering grandeur of the Himalayas.

Kathmandu was full of Hindu and Buddhist temples and stupas and was known as the City of Temples. It was a magnet for European and American hippies searching for the ultimate spiritual experience, many of them having travelled on the Magic Bus that offered transport from Istanbul to Kathmandu for €70 US, and quite a few had stayed and set up small cafés and bakeries that did a good trade in cakes and hash brownies. The menu in these establishments normally consisted mainly of British café fare – cup of tea, bacon and eggs, beans on toast etc. at very reasonable prices. For an extra half a rupee you could have any of these with hashish. We were staying in one of many tourist lodges situated in the city centre, which served porridge for breakfast. This made quite a pleasant change – at least on the first morning of our stay. While in Kathmandu I always had an unsettled stomach and consequently never had much appetite. I later learnt this was probably due to altitude sickness, the city being some 4,600 feet above sea level.

We spent a few days wandering around, taking in the unique atmosphere of this mountain kingdom before heading off back to the Indian border. We travelled back through Bihar, stopping overnight in Muzaffarpur, and then on into East Bengal, eventually arriving and getting a very warm welcome at Guntaj's parent's house. We spent a very pleasant evening enjoying delicious home cooking and recounting our journey since we had last seen him and his father in Delhi, before heading off quite late the next morning in the hope of making it to Calcutta by nightfall. However, the road was slow going and we were forced to stop and set up camp in pitch darkness at the side of the road outside the industrial city of Durgapur. Stu slept in the Transit to save putting his tent up, but in the morning his feet, which had been uncovered, were a mass of mosquito bites. These would become badly infected over the next few weeks. We learnt later that we had been extremely lucky not to have been attacked, as the spot where we had stopped was in the middle of a Communist-dominated area that was very anti-British.

Arriving in Calcutta we booked into the Fairlawns Hotel opposite the Salvation Army hostel in Sudder Street. The hotel was owned by a retired Indian Army colonel and his wife; it was a two-star "luxury" left-over from the British Raj, with beautifully manicured lawns and a bar that was well endowed with a good selection of gins and whiskies. The lady of the house was certainly a relic of the Raj, dressing for "afternoon tea", which seemed to consist mainly of gin and tonic, and referring to our Australian contingent as "You bloody colonials!"

The group gradually dispersed over the next few days, heading off home to Australia and New Zealand. As we awaited the arrival of our new group for the return trip, Stu and I decided to explore the city's sights and indulge in some shopping sorties to the local markets, culminating in Stu buying a sitar. In order to transport it safely back to the UK he had a substantial wooded box made for it, which was ceremoniously unloaded from the roof rack at every stop on the return trip, with the locals reverently watching, thinking it was a coffin!

***

A week later, we had our full complement of passengers, mostly young Australians travelling to Europe for the first time and a couple of Kiwis, plus Michelle and Peter. Having collected my trip funds for the return trip (£165) from American Express and got the Transit fully serviced, we set off on our return journey, retracing our steps back up to Kathmandu, down to Benares, on to Khajuraho (enjoying the delights of Mrs Jain's cooking once again) and through to Agra and then Delhi.

After crossing the border into Pakistan we travelled through to Peshawar and stayed overnight at the Dak bungalows. The next morning it was discovered that Stu's passport had been stolen from under his pillow while he slept. I hate to think what might have happened had he woken and caught the thief in the act, as life was very cheap in that part of the world and Stu could have ended up with a knife between his ribs. It was decided that he should travel on public transport back to the British High Commission in Islamabad to get a new passport while I took the group through to Kabul where we would wait for him to join us – which he did six days later, fraught and travel-weary.

I was driving down Chicken Street a couple of days into our stay when someone jumped into the road, wildly waving their arms. I thought it was some hippie high on hashish and didn't stop, but as I drove past, he called out, "Steve!" I slammed on the brakes and was thrilled to suddenly recognise Peter Fischer, who I'd last seen the previous summer in Heraclizia. Apparently Tebbi (his girlfriend), had met up with some people who were heading off to India for the winter and had decided to join them. Peter had felt at a great loss after she left and had decided to take to the Hippie Trail himself to try and find her, so far to no avail. The following day we loaded the group and a few friends of Peter's into the minibus and drove up to the Kabul Gorge before going "off piste" down a dusty track and spending the day on the shores of a beautiful azure-blue lake, swimming and drying off in the warm late-spring sunshine. I never saw or heard from Peter again after leaving Kabul, although I did hear a couple of years later that he had bought a horse and ridden through the tribal highlands, right across the north of Afghanistan.

We travelled back to the Iranian border crossing – an anxious time for me, as anyone found carrying hashish or any other drugs would be thrown into jail, or if it exceeded a certain amount, taken away and shot – irrespective of what nationality they were. I always made this clear to my passengers, telling them that if they were carrying anything, to get rid of it before we got to the border, as I would be held responsible for any drugs found on the bus, would result in me being taken away and the Transit confiscated – leaving them stranded. Fortunately, I never had this problem, although I did have one friend, Willard, who was arrested and eventually died in an Iranian jail.

We continued back through Iran, Turkey and Greece and then drove along the Dalmatian coast of Yugoslavia to Italy, stopping a couple of nights at Camping Fusina, before continuing up over the Brenner Pass to Innsbruck, and on through Austria, Germany and Belgium, arriving at Camping Lac Loppem on the outskirts of Bruges 97 days after leaving the UK. Pat Russell was in residence, as he'd been tasked with setting up a "European

Base Camp" for Frontier in order to save the cost of transporting the minibuses back and forwards across the channel. Instead, groups were being bought across as foot passengers and collected from the ferry port at Zeebrugge. He asked if I could do him a favour and take a Russia trip out that weekend, as he was a driver short. I pointed out (quite firmly), that I had just spent the last 14 weeks driving 21,000 miles to India and back and that all I wanted to do was get back to "Blighty" for a rest, some fish-and-chips and a pint of Watney's Red Barrel - so no, I wouldn't be taking the Russia trip!

We caught the ferry back to Dover the next morning. Stu was in a pretty bad state by now having broken out into a fever; his mosquito-bitten feet had become infected through his constant scratching. He subsequently spent several days recovering in hospital. As for myself – well I had a few days recuperation in Brighton, before reporting back for duty at Frontier's offices in Crawley.

9. THE SUMMER OF '71

After a few days recuperating, I was back on the road, spending most of that summer running trips to Greece and Turkey, with a couple of Moroccan excursions thrown into the mix. Frontier had taken on one driver, Micky Eckersly, who had experience with another overland company, but had come with a reputation for being "a bit unreliable". I was given the task of sounding him out as my co-driver on a couple of trips.

Micky was half Irish, half Scouse, a likeable character with a good sense of fun who got on well with the passengers – but he wasn't a good driver. Our first trip together found us travelling down to Greece. Now I'm not a good passenger; I prefer to drive, but having driven down through Belgium, Germany and Austria I asked Micky if he'd like to take the wheel for a while on the Zagreb/Belgrade stretch while I grabbed 40 winks which fortunately was only 40 winks, as on waking, I found him nodding off at the wheel. He never drove one of my buses again.

However, Frontier had opened an office in Rotterdam and, in order to cope with the unexpectedly large number of bookings, had contracted out to a Belgian coach company to run coach trips down to Morocco using Frontier drivers as couriers. So, the next trip Micky and I undertook together was on one of these trips as couriers – a two week run to Marrakesh, then back to Belgium, with 35 Dutch passengers. On reaching Marrakesh, Micky and I shared an annex in the basement of the Mahmoud hotel. One of our passengers was quite a skillful guitar player, who we invited back to our room for a music and drinking session, together with a few others and an American student, Tammy, who Micky had met that afternoon. She was on a weekend break from Casablanca, where she was on a student exchange course.

On the quayside in Algeciras - summer '71

Everyone had drifted off to their rooms by about 3.00am, except for Tammy and Anna, one of the Dutch girls from the trip. Anna joined me in my bed on one side of the room, while Micky and Tammy proceeded to jump into his bed on the other side. Within a few minutes, judging by the noises coming from their side of the room (loud grunting and groaning), there was a lot of activity going on and a considerable amount of energy being expended.

I woke at 8am to find that Anna and I were alone in the room. Micky re-appeared late that afternoon looking pale, drawn and very nervous.

"Has she gone - the American?" he asked.

"As far as I know – I haven't seen her," I replied.

He looked intensely relieved and, as he began to relax with the help of a couple of cold beers, he explained how the previous night had unfolded for him. As soon as they were in bed Tammy had made it abundantly clear that she wasn't interested in sleeping; she wanted sex – and Micky responded with great enthusiasm and, from the sound of it, great athleticism. About 20 minutes later, Micky was lying there ready to go to sleep after his exertions, when Tammy whispered that she wanted to "do it again". It transpired that her record for the number of times she had had sex in a single night was eight! and she wanted to try and break her record – which apparently, they had, leaving Micky absolutely shattered! Tammy had to be back at her hotel before the teacher in charge of her group discovered that she had been out all night, so Micky escorted her to said hotel, promising as they parted to see her again before she left for the return journey to Casablanca later that afternoon – which of course he never did.

Micky had a message from Frontier a couple of months later telling him that Tammy had been in touch with them and was trying to contact him, as she was pregnant and her father (who was apparently a Texan oil millionaire) was insisting that he should marry her. Nothing ever came of it, but he was running scared for a while with visions of an angry Texan father hunting him down, followed by a shotgun wedding.

Frontier decided to give Micky one more chance, as the increase in passenger numbers was impacting on them and they had discovered that there was a shortage of experienced drivers, so our next trip took us back down to Morocco. Having crossed from Spain to Ceuta, we stocked up with a couple of crates of Johnny Walker to sell in Tangier at a profit of £1 per bottle. This was "good money"; as an "experienced driver", I was being paid the grand sum of £18 a week by now. On the second night in Tangier we took the passengers to the Tangerine Bar, which was run by a couple of ex-pats, Liz and Johnny. I mentioned that we had the whiskey on board if they were interested, which they were. They told us to wait until things quietened down a bit before we bought it in.

So, about midnight Micky and I went to the bus parked opposite the bar, took the two crates from the back, crossed the road and back into the bar, not noticing the two men following close behind us who turned out to be plain-clothes police. The whiskey was confiscated and Micky was taken into custody, while I, having explained that I had to take my group of "tourists" back to the campsite, was told to report, with the minibus, to the local police station early the next morning. I drove the passengers, who were unaware of the evening's unfortunate developments, back and then set off early the next morning before they surfaced. The bus was impounded while the police gave it a thorough search for more illicit alcohol, drugs, etc. and I was told to report back later that afternoon.

On returning to the campsite the passengers wanted to know where the bus was; thinking on my feet, I told them I had taken it to a garage for some repair work. Some of them asked if I could I take them to the garage, as they needed to retrieve their cameras from the bus. Still thinking on my feet, I explained that it had been discovered that there was a problem with the electrics and the garage had taken the bus to an auto-electrician to get it fixed – but I didn't know where that was!

At 4.00pm both the bus and a pale-looking Micky were released. We could continue our journey down to Marrakech and back, but I would have to pay a fine of 200 dirham (about £20) before we were allowed to leave the country. On our return to Tangier, I had to ask Johnny to lend me the money to pay the fine, as my funds were somewhat stretched after paying for the whiskey in Ceuta. I later discovered that Johnny had known the bar was being watched by the police, but hadn't bothered to tell me. In retrospect, I wouldn't be surprised if he had then bought the Scotch back from the police at a lower price than I would have asked for; it's the way things worked back then.

***

As Micky was not the most responsible of people, he didn't last long at Frontier. However, he managed to find employment with various other overland companies over the next couple of years, but stories of his crazy escapades kept surfacing. Towards the end of the summer, I had a group that included quite a number of Dutch passengers from Frontier's Rotterdam office. I was sitting on the beach at George's Taverna in Heraclizia chatting with some of the group, relating anecdotes about trips I'd made earlier in the year and happened to mention Micky's name. One of the Dutch lads immediately started shaking, muttering "No, no, no!" He eventually calmed down (with the help of a large ouzo) and explained that he had been on a Greek trip with another company the previous year and Micky had been the driver. "He was mad! He tried to drive our minibus up Mount Olympus and there was no road and it was very rocky and we had a puncture. He left us to go and find help and it was getting dark – and there were wolves out there!" It had obviously been quite a traumatic experience for him.

A year or so later, Frank McGrath (of Safari fame) and his lovely wife Jackie had set up their own travel company running trips down to Greece. They had made their Greek base at the campsite on the island of Thassos, the most northerly of all the Greek islands, situated off the coast near Kavala. Micky had turned up with a group at the campsite on a Saturday evening. The next day Frank organized a party for the various groups staying on the site, which involved a BBQ, music and quite a lot of alcohol. Late that afternoon, Micky's minibus was seen leaving the campsite and Frank, on asking where he had gone, was told that Micky had decided to take his girlfriend for a drive to the small town on the far side of the island, along the one road on the island that linked the two towns. Later that evening Micky and his girlfriend walked into the campsite, explaining that they had got half way to the other town. However, they had then decided to turn back, as it was beginning to get dark and he had, in the process of executing a three-point turn, "backed the minibus into a ditch".

It was getting late, so Frank decided to take another minibus the next morning and tow his Transit out of the ditch. However, on arriving at the scene, they found that he had actually it backed over the side of a cliff and it was only the fact that he'd hit a tree a few feet down the cliff face that had stopped the bus from plunging all the way down and into the sea! The biggest tow-truck in Kavala had to be bought over on the ferry in order to drag the bus back up onto the road. I don't think Micky's overland career lasted much longer after that little incident.

Colin Payten contacted me that August. Another India trip was due to depart early in September and he had a potential problem with one particular Australian passenger, Kathy O'Connor, who was due to take the trip on her way back home to Oz. She had been on a Russia and Scandinavia trip with Frontier earlier in the year (possibly the one that I had turned down), but apparently the driver had never driven that route before. Bear in mind that, ,according to the brochure, "Our driver/leaders …..have done their route many times, know the snags and how to by-pass them". The trip had been a complete disaster, so on her return she contacted Colin and explained in no uncertain terms that, if she turned up at Victoria coach station to board the minibus only to discover that the designated driver had never driven the India route before she would: *a)* not board the bus, and: *b)* sue Frontier for everything she could get out of them. Gus and Micky Hynes, the only other drivers to have done the trip, weren't interested – so I was his last resort other than trying to recruit an India-experienced driver from another company, which would be difficult in such a short space of time. I'd enjoyed the first trip, had made some good friends en route and so I agreed, but with a little bit of trepidation regarding this "Kathy" person.

10. İNDİA 2

September arrived, and it transpired that, due to the number of bookings for the trip, we were to run two Transits, with each bus taking about eight passengers; the second bus was to be driven by "rookie" Clive Fennimore, a university student who was taking time out from his studies and had been working for Frontier during the summer. The outward journey was to be Clive's training trip with me as lead driver and his guiding light. I was told that Ms O'Connor, the Australian who had been the reason for me undertaking my 2nd India trip that year, had to be on my bus. I must admit that I had just a little bit of consternation about how the trip might develop with a potentially awkward passenger aboard and my heart sank when I first set eyes on someone who, to look at, was the female equivalent of the Australian comedy actor, Sid James. However, it soon became apparent that my fears were unfounded. Kathy turned out to be one of the best passengers I ever had the pleasure of travelling with.

A few days into the trip, having driven down through Europe, we were in Northern Greece heading for the Turkish border when we spotted a hitch-hiker with a Union Jack on their backpack. "Shall we stop and give them a lift?" I enquired. "Yeah", came the response - led by Kathy - "it'll be a bit of fresh blood - someone new to talk to!" So, we stopped and took on-board a young lady in her early twenties by the name of Brenda, ("call me Bren"). She was a policeman's daughter from Devon, who was hitch-hiking down to India in order to spend the winter in Goa. Bren started chatting away and it transpired that this was the third year she had done the trip, as apparently you could rent a beach bungalow with a cook and a housemaid that would sleep eight people, for the grand sum of £25 a month. She was meeting up with a couple of travelling companions in Istanbul and they were hoping to continue the journey together down to India - although getting lifts for three people together would be difficult.

We arrived late afternoon in Camping Londra on the outskirts of Istanbul, set up the tents and went to a local kebab house for food and drinks. Bren was getting on famously with the group and by the time we wandered back to the campsite, she and I had decided to share a tent for the night.

I took the group into the city the next morning and later that day met up with Bren's two travelling companions, Johanna - a Dutch girl about the same age as Bren, who had also done the trip before - and Jasmine Gaston - a young South African girl aged 18 who had met Bren in England and was doing the trip for the first time. As the group and I sat with the three girls in the Pudding Shop that evening it was suggested (probably by me) that, as we had plenty of room in the minibus and our new-found friends were good company, maybe we could give them a lift right the way through to Delhi - and so it came to pass.

After a couple of days in Istanbul Bren was getting on like a house on fire with Kathy and had introduced her (unbeknownst to me at the time) to Benzedrine, an amphetamine known as "bennies" or "uppers", which you could buy over the counter in Turkey. As we were due to travel down to the south coast, Mustafa from the leather shop asked if I could give him a lift as far as Balikesir, where, on arrival, we decided to stop and camp for the night beside an auto-stop outside the town.

The group hit the bar that evening and were introduced to the "pleasures" of raki, the Turkish equivalent of ouzo, by Mustafa who was enjoying the company. Bren, who had obviously dropped a couple of bennies and wasn't holding back on the raki, was getting very loud and making some rather controversial remarks. I decided it was time to disappear and headed back to the tent for an early night. About twenty minutes later I heard her coming across the campsite, looking for me and shouting in a slurred voice.

"Where are you, you bastard - I'm going to find you and grind you!" The tent flap was un-zipped and she crawled in and started shaking me, demanding, "Wake up – wake up you bastard!" I decided that I was going to feign a deep sleep no matter what, and eventually she collapsed beside me and went to sleep, much to my relief. I think that was the first and possibly only time I have been scared of a woman - and that was the last night I shared a tent with Bren.

***

We dropped Mustapha in the city the next morning and continued down to the south coast. Finding a deserted beach alongside the road, the group decided that they would like a final dip in the Aegean, as it was the last time they would see the sea on our trip. To avoid unpacking the roof rack to access their swimming gear, everyone rushed into the sea wearing their shorts, T-shirts, etc. I was sitting with Bren at the top of the beach watching the group enjoying themselves, when I became captivated by the sight of Jasmine, a vision of beauty and innocence, as she left the water and walked up the beach with her thin cotton blouse clinging to her body. Bren watched Jasmine and then, glancing in my direction, delivered an ultimatum – "You go near her - and I'll ruin this trip for you!" I realised straight away that this was a threat that was not to be dismissed lightly.

So, the trip continued with the threat of sabotage hanging over me, through Turkey, Iran and then into Afghanistan where, on our second day in the country, we stopped for an overnight stay at a small hotel in Kandahar that Bren had used before. Sitting in the hotel café that evening, Bren kept glancing at a black man at the end of the bar who looked up as she asked, "Aren't you Abdul – Abdul No-Sweat?"

"Yeah man – hey – you're Big Bren! I remember you man – I met you in Goa last year!" and with that Abdul No-Sweat came and joined us.

"Which way are you headed?", he asked on discovering that I was the driver of an overland trip.

"We're heading for Kabul tomorrow", I replied.

"Hey man, no sweat – me too!"

"That's great – maybe we can travel in convoy".

"I don't know man – I'll be leaving real early, like five o'clock, but I'll be getting to Kabul a lot later than you".

"Why's that?"

"Well, I've got my old VW Kombi – you probably saw it parked outside - the one with flowers painted all over it. You see, I don't pay the tolls man. I stop at each toll post and just have a glass of tea with the guy at the toll – and share a spliff with him. That's why I'll get to Kabul after you, because I drive real slow when I'm stoned, man".

"What? You drive when you're stoned?"

"Yeah man, I only drive when I'm stoned - otherwise I hit things! So, where you staying in Kabul?"

"On my last trip we stayed at the Green Hotel in Chicken Street".

"Oh no man – that's a dump! Go to the Mustafa Hotel; it might cost you an extra five Afghani a night, but it's much better."

"OK – maybe see you in Kabul".

We arrived in Kabul late the following afternoon and promptly checked in to the Mustafa Hotel – which was quite a bit better that the Green Hotel, as Abdul had said. Early next morning, as I lay half asleep, I heard my bedroom door open and there was Abdul.

"Hey, mornin' man – I bought you a spliff".

"Piss off Abdul! I don't want a spliff - it's only seven o'clock and I'm still asleep!"

"No sweat man, I leave you a lump. See you at breakfast", and with that he left about an ounce of hashish on my bedside table. This turned out to be a re-occurring theme over the next few days – with an ever-increasing pile of hash accumulating on my bedside table.I eventually got down to breakfast about nine o'clock to find Abdul sitting there with a glass of tea and rolling a jumbo-sizes spliff using a patchwork of cigarette papers. Apparently, he had arrived in Kabul quite late the previous evening, as, apart from his extended stops at the toll posts, he had picked up the MD of the local Coca Cola factory and his family whose car had broken down, and given them a lift into the city.

Over the next few days in Abdul's company, I learnt that he was Nigerian and had taken a degree in economics in England, then travelled around Europe and Scandinavia before eventually settling in Afghanistan about three years earlier. Apparently, he had got to know a number of high-ranking military officers, enabling him to fly to most places in the country on military aircraft; he made his living by travelling to remote areas, buying tribal rugs and then flying to Hong Kong to sell them. With the money he made, he bought cheap watches and electrical gadgets which he then sold at a profit back in Kabul. Abdul kept asking me when I was going to sell my minibus.

"I can't sell the minibus; I've got my passengers to look after and I have to get them to Calcutta!"

"Yeah man – all the best drivers sell their bus here or in Kathmandu!"

"Well, I'm sorry, but I'm not doing it".

I think, at that moment, I was a bit of a disappointment to Abdul.

Sitting in the 25 Hour club one evening, Abdul and I were enjoying a meal when a young man walked in.

"Keep your head down!" said Abdul, "I know him - that's one of the Princes – the younger one! I don't want him to see me man, as he's not the brightest of people, so he's always followed by bodyguards and secret police who make a note of everyone he speaks to - which can make for problems".

The prince glanced round the restaurant and, on spotting us. immediately called out, "Hi Abdul – can I join you?"

"Sure – no sweat man", Abdul reluctantly replied - and he came across and sat down at our table – much to Abdul's discomfort.

I was introduced and we chatted for a while before the prince announced that a new ten-pin bowling alley, the first in the country, had recently opened in the city and we should join him for a game the following day. Which is how, in October 1971 I ended up going ten-pin bowling with the Prince of Afghanistan, who turned out to be a pleasant young man and good company.

A day before we were due to leave Kabul, Jasmine and Johanna decided they would be leaving us, as they wanted to travel to central Afghanistan to visit the famous giant Buddhas that had been carved into the side of a cliff in the Bamiyan Valley. We said our goodbyes, before continuing our trip through Pakistan, into India and on to New Delhi, where Bren announced she was off to meet up with her Indian boyfriend (the first time she'd actually mentioned him) before heading off with him to Goa. I was quite relieved to see the back of her, due to her ever-threatening presence and the shadow she had cast over the trip for me.

***

A few days later we were travelling on country roads through Central Northern India on our way to Benares when the Transit began to lose power, as the engine started coughing and spluttering. I pulled over to the side of the road, got out and lifted the bonnet. I checked the spark plugs and points, which seemed fine and came to the conclusion that we must have picked up some dirty fuel, meaning the carburettor jets were probably blocked. Having dismantled the top of the carburettor, I asked one of the passengers to turn on the ignition and turn the engine over in order to flush the jets through. There must have been a stray spark somewhere, as the next thing I knew the engine was engulfed in flames. I rushed round to the passenger door and shouted, "Quick everyone out – the engines on fire!" They thought I was being my usual jokey self and just sat there chuckling until I grabbed a towel and rushed back to the front of the bus to smother the flames.

Having put the fire out, I surveyed the damage and discovered the heat had melted the solder on the copper float (the part that controls and maintains the level of fuel flow into the carburetor), which now lay trampled and in 3 pieces on the ground. Clive pulled up behind me in the second Transit as I stood there with singed eyebrows, contemplating the damage and trying to figure out how I was going to get my bus back up and running. We had passed through a small village a few miles back along the road, so I asked Clive to take the pieces and try to find someone in the village who could straighten them out and maybe solder the float back together again.

It was a long shot, but two hours later he returned with a somewhat battered, but reconstructed float. I re-assembled the carburetor and lo-and-behold, managed to start the engine! However, when I tried to pull away there was no throttle. On lifting the bonnet once again I soon discovered that the plastic outer covering on the throttle cable had been melted by the fire, which meant that, when the accelerator pedal was compressed, the outer cable was concertinaing, instead of the inner cable moving and operating the throttle. Plucking a couple of stout twigs from a roadside bush and using a roll of sticking plaster from the first-aid kit, I made a splint for the damaged section of the cable. It worked and my temporary repair job actually took us not only onward to Calcutta via Kathmandu, but all the way back to the UK!

We continued on into Nepal. On the day before we were due to leave Kathmandu for the last leg to Calcutta, Kathy – who had become the life and soul of the group - came to see me. She explained, "I want to finish the trip and see Calcutta – but I'd really like to spend more time in Nepal". I thought for a couple of minutes and then came up with a suggestion. "How about coming to Calcutta and then coming back to Kathmandu with the new group? You can act as courier to help ease them in and explain to them what to expect on their trip to the UK". And so it was agreed.

The following morning, we were heading back through the Himalayan foothills to the Indian border when I became aware that the Transit was behaving strangely; it somehow seemed lopsided. I pulled over to the side of the road and after jacking up the bus I climbed underneath to investigate, quickly identifying the problem to be a broken leaf on a rear suspension spring. Clive had pulled in behind me and after a short discussion, it was decided that I would dismantle the broken spring unit, then Clive would then drive back to Kathmandu to try to find a replacement. After Clive had left, we proceeded to set up camp on the side of a valley; after a while a number of children from the small farms further down the valley gradually gathered. They shyly kept their distance and chatted excitedly amongst themselves, watching us as we set up the camping stoves, put the kettles on and took a large catering tin of instant coffee from the bus. As we took the tin lid from the coffee tin the children started laughing, gesticulating and backing away from us. We realized that the shiny tin lid was like a mirror – maybe something they had never seen before. Or perhaps they were fearful of it, based on some local folklore or superstition. As dusk approached and we cooked up a meal from our emergency food store of dehydrated catering meals, the children gradually dispersed and we could hear their singing rising up from the valley as they headed back to their farms. Clive arrived the following afternoon, having found a blacksmith in Kathmandu who had fashioned and fitted a new leaf to the spring unit, which I was able to fit back on the bus before we headed off to the Indian border and on to Calcutta.

***

In order to save me carrying large amounts of money on the outward trip, Frontier would give me the trip funds for the outer leg and then send money for the return leg to Calcutta via American Express. However, on this occasion no funds had arrived prior to our departure date from Calcutta; according to a telex message from Pat Russell, this was due to a "glitch" at American Express. He asked if I could I perhaps borrow some money from the passengers to get us up to Kathmandu, where he would arrange for Amex to forward the funds for me. The new group of just 12 passengers, split between the two minibuses, were none too happy about the situation, but reluctantly agreed to provide temporary funding to get us on our way.

It transpired that it would be Clive's birthday while we were in Kathmandu, so on arriving, we decided to take the biggest room in the lodge where we were staying and have a party for him with our new group. On his birthday, Kathy and I went into the city, returning with a large hash cake which we cut up into chunks and, as the un-suspecting passengers arrived that evening clutching their bottles of KAT 69 whisky and Kukri rum, we offered them a piece of Clive's "birthday cake". After a while, with music playing on my cassette player, Kathy and I were sitting on the floor in the centre of the room sharing a chillum and in fits of giggles as our party guests began to remark that their heads felt "funny", having munched away on what was a very tasty cake, washed down with, what they concluded, was "shit strong local brew!" It was a good party.

When the time came to leave Kathmandu and say goodbye to Kathy, no money had arrived (PR: "Don't know what Amex are doing – can you make it down to Delhi and I'll get them to transfer funds there"). Speaking with Kathy that evening,

I remarked on how it was going to be difficult to ask the passengers for another loan. Straight away she offered to lend me the money for the trip to Delhi – as long as she got it back on her return to Australia, and I gratefully accepted her offer. I honestly don't know to this day whether Kathy ever got her money back from Frontier, but I hope she did.

We arrived in Delhi to find no funds – still, apparently, a problem with Amex. I was told that if Frontier couldn't get money to me before I left, they would arrange for Amex to forward it to Tehran. I still had a bit of Kathy's loan left, but it wasn't going to get the group and two Transits even as far as Kabul, let alone Tehran. I began to think that, if worst came to worst, I might have to consider Abdul's suggestion of selling one of the minibuses.

Driving into Connaught Place the next morning, I saw a Frontier bus parked up. I pulled over, wandered across and found Matt Davies, my old friend from the Nomad Travelers' Club, slumped on a back seat and looking terrible; he was very thin, pale and in dire need of a shower. It transpired that he'd been asked to take the next India trip after mine, which had turned into a nightmare. Apparently, Frontier had been having "cash flow problems" before he left the UK, so they had provided him with trip funds to get him to Turkey, with the promise that funds for the remainder of the trip would be made available when he reached Istanbul. This started to sound a bit familiar to me. Pat Russell had flown down to rendezvous with Matt and had given him the remainder of his trip funds in Pakistani 50 Rupee notes, money that Gus and Micky had bought back from their India trip (for whatever reason – possibly because they were able to buy them very cheaply on the black market in Kabul). Unknown to Matt, these notes had been withdrawn as legal tender a couple of months earlier due to the number of forgeries that were circulating in that part of the world.

Russell had presumably been well aware of this when he handed over the money and scooted off back to the UK. On discovering that the notes were worthless when he came to change some of them for Turkish Lira, Matt had had to ask his passengers to fund the trip until he could arrange proper financing from Frontier. On reaching Kabul, with no further trip funds forthcoming, he had become seriously ill with amoebic dysentery and been admitted to the local hospital. Matt told me, "It had a dirt floor, there was no food provided and every morning they would carry out the bodies of people who had died during the night, over their shoulders. Although I was feeling terrible, I thought if I didn't discharge myself, the only way I would be leaving the hospital was over someone's shoulder".

The only affordable accommodation Matt had been able to find in Delhi with his limited finances was quite squalid – dirty and with no proper washing facilities, so we headed back to our hostel in New Delhi for him to have a decent shower, before heading off for a decent meal. By the time I left him to go and meet back with his group, he was looking 100% better. Years later, Matt told me that he had been at a very low ebb and he reckoned that I'd saved his life that day. Needless to say, he left Frontier at the end of that trip and continued his overland career with various other companies over the next few years. We're still good friends to this day.

***

I was driving round Connaught Place on our final day when unbelievably, in a city, at that time, of around three and a half million people, I suddenly spotted Jasmine walking along the pavement. I pulled to the side of the road and shouted above the cacophony of blaring horns from taxis and tuk-tuks, for her to jump in. It transpired that after she had returned to Kabul after visiting Bamiyan with Joanna and had met some people who had offered her $1,000 to take a suitcase to Australia for them via Karachi. Literally an innocent abroad, she didn't realize that these people were drug-runners that would find naïve, good-looking girls that were on the hippy trail, dress them in kinky boots and a miniskirt and then pay them to carry a suitcase with several kilos of hashish sandwiched between layers of fiberglass built into it, to be handed to a contact in Australia. Jasmine had flown into Sydney, delivered her suitcase, and had then spent some time on her return journey in the hippy Shangri-La of Bali before flying into Delhi that morning. She was on her way back to Kabul – so I offered her a lift, which she gratefully accepted.

That afternoon I was parked in Connaught Place waiting for my passengers to return from their final sightseeing/shopping sortie when I was approached by a young man who asked, "Which way are you headed – Kathmandu, or back to Europe?"

"Europe" I replied.

"Would you like to make yourself $100?".

"Maybe – it depends".

"My boss has some merchandise that he needs to get to Kabul – no drugs involved. My name is Sanj. Be here at six o'clock this evening and I'll take you to meet him; he will explain everything".

I was desperate for money and $100 would certainly get the two Transits to Tehran if we were careful and we had no emergencies on route, so there I was that evening waiting in Connaught Place when the young man called Sanj, appeared right on time. He climbed into the bus and directed me to an area of Old Delhi where we parked. Sanj led me down some narrow alleys before passing through a door, across a small courtyard and into a house to meet his boss – a very large Sikh gentleman who was reclining on a bed of cushions. He motioned for me to sit and then announced that we would eat first before we talked business. He shouted some orders and a timid looking woman (his wife?) started to bring beautiful, fragrant dishes to a low table in the centre of the room – this man obviously enjoyed his food! We sat cross legged around the table and ate with our fingers, using chapatis and roti to scoop up the food.

When we'd finished eating, "the boss" announced that we would go to inspect the items that he wanted me to transport for him. We went back to where the Transit was parked and, after a short drive, entered a compound where his goods were stored. He indicated a number of sacks stacked under a lean-to against a wall, telling me, "A few of these are filled with silk that you will drop off in the Khyber Pass and the rest are sacks of stone for Kabul".

"Stone?" I queried.

"Yes. We just pick up as much of this as we want in the desert in Rajasthan. They use it to make graves in Afghanistan, where it's very expensive – so it's good business for me! You can check all the sacks if you want; there are no drugs – just as I told you".

I checked a few sacks; when I was satisfied that they were "clean" his men loaded them onto the roof rack.

"How will I know where to drop these things off?" I asked. He indicated the men that had been loading the Transit.

"One of these boys will be waiting for you in the Khyber and will flag you down. Another one will contact you when you reach Kabul".

As he handed over $100 US in crisp $5 notes, he explained that, if I got stopped by customs at the Pakistan border, I should just leave the goods there and he would arrange for them to be collected later by one of his men. (Obviously a few dollars would exchange hands between his employee and the Pakistani customs officials) and I could keep the $100 he had paid me. I felt quite relieved and rather pleased with myself as I headed back to New Delhi with my newly acquired funds sitting in my pocket.

There were some puzzled looks the next morning as the passengers tried to find room to stow their suitcases on, what was now a rather cramped roof rack. After some moaning about the lack of space I managed to jam everything in, explaining that I was "just carrying a few things through to Kabul for a friend" and we eventually left for the Pakistan border crossing with a somewhat bulging canvas retaining the contents of the roof rack. We cleared Pakistani customs with no problem, but as it was getting late, decided to camp that night beside the border post. That night Jasmine and I slept together on the roof rack with our sleeping bags zipped together under the stars – and I fell in love again.

Two days later, we were travelling from Islamabad to Peshawar when I felt the rear spring give way again (probably under the weight of the excess baggage being carried). Climbing under the bus once more, I dismantled the spring unit and gave it to Clive, asking him to carry on into Peshawar to try and find a replacement. I told the passengers to get back in the bus while we were waiting for Clive to return and lock the doors, as a crowd of men quickly gathered around us. Some of them kept trying to open the doors – while a couple of local policemen just stood at the back of the crowd and watched. I eventually got out to confront the gathering and was told by one of them that they just wanted our women! Clive returned about three hours later with a new spring unit that he'd located in a scrap yard. (Fortunately, Ford Transit minibuses were common in Pakistan at that time, as they were a popular form of local transport). I climbed back under the bus while the crowd continued to mill around, tripping over my outstretched legs as I worked to refit the spring unit. With the job done we moved on to Peshawar.

The following day found us driving up through the Khyber Pass towards the Afghan border at Landi Kotal, when I spotted a man sitting on a rock at the side of the road who, on seeing the Transit approaching, stepped out in front of the minibus and waved us down. Sure enough, he was one of the men who had helped load the roof rack in Delhi.

"You have the silk from Delhi, yes?" he asked, as he opened the front passenger door and sat down in the seat beside me.

"Yes, of course" I replied.

"OK, we need to go this way" he said, indicating a dirt track leading off the main road to the right. The passengers were becoming anxious as I followed the track winding up into the hills.

"Where are we going, driver?" they asked – probably with visions of kidnapping beginning to materialize.

"It's OK" I assured them, "I just have to drop a couple of things off for my friend".

After about a kilometer we came to a Pashtun village, stopping beside one of the flat roofed, mud brick houses. The sacks of silk were duly unloaded before my "friend" guided us back to the main road and waved us on our way.

I drove on to Kabul and about ten minutes after booking into the Mustafa Hotel I was told someone was waiting for me in reception. It was another of the men from Delhi who directed me to a compound on the edge of the city where the sacks of rock were unloaded. I headed back to the hotel where I found Jasmine waiting for me. She seemed on edge and explained that she had to report back to the people who had recruited her for the trip to Australia, but she would try to see me before I left.

I was passing the Metropole Hotel the next morning when I noticed (another) Frontier Transit parked outside. I went in and enquired whether the driver of the minibus was staying in the hotel. "Room 301", I was told. I took the stairs, wandered down the corridor and knocked on the door.

"Yeah – come in", I heard.

Inside I found one of my fellow drivers, Bertie Samkiss, lying on the bed with a young lady who turned out to be his Kiwi girlfriend. Bertie wasn't your "standard" macho overland driver (and neither was I, come to that); he was a short, tubby and bespectacled Mancunian. The last time I'd seen him had been the previous summer at a campsite in Asilah, south of Tangier, when he had been wearing a shabby blue djellaba and smoking a spliff. After exchanging man-hugs and chatting for a while, I explained that Ali Shiraz was throwing a party for my group that evening and invited Bertie and his lady to join us.

"Hmm – not sure we'll be able to. We've been eating that stuff", he replied, indicating a lump of hashish on the bedside table, "and I'm not sure what effect it's going to have on us".

"What – in brownies, or something?" I asked.

"No, just as it is" he said, "like chocolate!"

Nevertheless, they did turn up at the party that evening, where we drank, smoked and enjoyed the food that Ali had arranged to be sent up from the club. I saw Bertie the following morning and asked if he'd enjoyed the party.

"Yeah, it was great" he replied "but don't ever do that to me again!"

"Do what?"

"Well, you were well stoned and sat in front of me for an hour explaining why the Irish were Irish. You completely blew my mind!"

The day before we were due to leave, Jasmine came to my room. Looking and sounding scared, she told me that it could be dangerous for me if she was seen talking to me.

"These people don't want us - me and the other girls - talking to anyone".

I implored her "Come with me back to the UK".

"I can't" she replied, "they're watching me all the time. Here – take this as a thank you for the lift," and she gave me the cassette of James Taylor's album *"Sweet Baby James"* that we had been playing continuously on the trip from Delhi.

"Maybe it will remind you of me".

I was devastated, but gave her my contact details in the UK; before kissing me goodbye, she took a small gold Turkish puzzle ring from her finger and slipped it on the little finger of my left hand. I played the James Taylor tape constantly on the trip back and the words of "Fire and Rain" stuck in my head:

I've seen fire and I've seen rain
I've seen sunny days that I thought would never end
I've seen lonely times when I could not find a friend
But I always thought that I'd see you again

With all the travelling I'd done over the previous two years it seemed to sum up my situation - and I just had a feeling that I *would* see Jasmine again.

***

A few days later, we arrived in Tehran hoping to collect our trip funds waiting for us at American Express – only to discover that there was no American Express in Tehran. The next morning, having eaten a breakfast of dates from a street market (all I could afford by this time), I visited the British Embassy and explained our situation to a sympathetic staff member, who promised to resolve the problem for me as quickly as possible. The next morning, two black-suited men from the Foreign Office walked into the Frontier office in Crawley to announce that the company had two minibuses with 12 British citizens on board stranded in Tehran with no trip funds and demanded that money be sent immediately. The next morning, funds arrived via the National Bank of Iran.

About a week later we drove into Northern Greece; after all the problems I had endured on the return trip, I felt a huge wave of relief as we arrived in Heraclizia. George's taverna on the beach was closed for the winter, so that evening we gathered in Theo's establishment in the village square, where we were joined by some of the local lads and a lot of drinking and dancing ensued; I was "home", back in Greece.

I eventually arrived back in the UK in mid-December. After bidding goodbye to my passengers at the now familiar Victoria Station coach terminal and checking in with Frontier, I made the short drive to my sister Margaret's house in Ilford for a well-deserved Christmas break, before heading back to Brighton for the New Year. A few days later, a very apologetic Colin Payten called me into the office. Frontier was to undertake a reconnaissance expedition across Africa - its' first-ever trans-Africa trip, using two long-wheel based Land Rovers with just enough passengers to cover the cost of the trip; Gus was to drive the lead vehicle and Colin asked if I would take the second. I accepted without hesitation. 1972 looked like it could be another very exciting year!

11. TRANS-AFRICA 1972

GETTING STARTED

The Africa expedition was scheduled to leave at the end of February for a return trip to Cape Town; Gus was to have a brand-new Land Rover with the latest Salisbury rear axle assembly, while I was to drive a 1964 model (sporting Spanish remold tyres), that Frontier had hired from George Gordon-Smith an ex-Safari drive. It needed a bit of upgrading and a roof rack fitted before it was ready to tackle the journey. Both vehicles were fitted with side-pods to carry jerry cans for fuel and water, and carried a good supply of tools and spare parts that might be needed. However, it was obvious, as the departure date approached, that the work on my vehicle would not be completed in time and it was decided that Gus should leave with the full contingent of nine passengers and give them an extended tour of Morocco while waiting for the necessary work on my LR to be completed. I would then drive straight down through France and Spain with minimal stops and rendezvous with them in Tangier.

I left a few days later, with some work still needed on my vehicle, and after a long, lonely journey on my own with just my music tapes to accompany me, I arrived in Tangier. As there was still some work required on the LR, I booked in to the White Bear Hotel, which was run by ex-Safari driver Peter Raphael, who also ran a local motor repair workshop where I could get the necessary work done. That afternoon I found myself sitting at the bar with a group of ex-pat gay men who met there on a daily basis to chat and play liar dice for bottles of Stork lager, together with a small, moustachioed Moroccan who was about a third of the way into a bottle of Scotch that was sitting on the bar beside him. I was invited to join in the game of dice while the lads sent the house boy out to buy fresh artichokes from the market. These were boiled and served up 45 minutes later with fresh mayonnaise as a dip.

Half way through the afternoon, during a lull in the dice game, I was approached by the rather inebriated Moroccan who flashed a police identity card at me and instructed me to step outside. There he announced that he was the Chief of Police and demanded to see my passport. On telling him that I didn't have it on me, he pulled a gun from a shoulder holster concealed under his jacket and, putting it under my chin, told me he was taking me to the police station for questioning. Thinking very quickly and feeling rather desperate, I blurted "But you've still got half a bottle to finish in there". He considered this for several seconds (although it seemed longer), before nodding his agreement, placing the gun back in its holster and staggering back into the hotel. The chief of police continued drinking for a while and eventually took the remaining quarter bottle and left the building - slowly and rather unsteadily. After he'd gone, my fellow dice players explained that he came most afternoons and was given a bottle of whiskey "to keep him sweet".

Towards the end of the afternoon, we were joined at the bar by Moulay, the dancer who had entertained us on my first trip to

Marrakesh as a passenger with Gus. Moulay liked to seek out the company of overland drivers in order to encourage them to bring their groups to watch him dance. He was pleased and surprised to find a driver in Tangier this early in the year and chatted for a while before heading off for his evening's work, asking, as he left if I would be around the following day.

I was engaged with another session of liar dice the next afternoon when Moulay wandered into the bar, came over to me and, with a big smile, slipped a small package into my hand. "A little gift for you – something I thought you might like", he announced. I opened the package to discover that Moulay had just given me a packet of kif, a local mixture of tobacco and dried marijuana. I panicked, having visions of being arrested again by my policeman friend, with a supply of kif in my possession. I rushed upstairs to my room, dived into the bathroom and proceeded to flush Moulay's kind gift down the toilet – which, being a dried substance, proved to be quite difficult and required increasingly desperate and repeated flushings before it eventually disappeared completely.

***

Gus arrived in Tangier with our passengers a few days later. There was Ian "Bettsie" Betts who was basically an Australian cowboy from upstate Victoria. He would herd cattle up into the High Country of the Great Dividing Range in the spring and then bring them down again in the autumn before the snows fell. In the winter he worked for the local town council, doing "whatever needs doing -mending fences, etc." Bettsie's best mate was Ken "Tricksy" Tryhorn; the two of them had endured isolation, heat and dust while working on road construction in the outback for several months to raise the money for their "trip of a lifetime". They were tough characters. Jim, another Australian, was from a wealthy family in Sydney and was a bit full of himself; he didn't get on well with his two compatriots. John was an American, a quiet man who tended to keep himself to himself, while Annastasia (Anna), was a Greek-American who smiled and talked a lot. Grant and his wife Helen, who had worked for a while as a nurse, were Canadians, as was Bill Kennedy and his friend Ben.

While we were waiting for the work on my LR to be finalized we met up with two Liverpudlians and their girlfriends, who were about to attempt their own trans-Africa trip in a VW Kombi. They had raised sponsorship for their trip from local businesses in and around Liverpool, with one pharmaceutical company donating a huge box full of yellow multi-vitamin tablets instead of actual money – a very ample supply of which they were delighted to offload onto us.

TRANS-SAHARA – ALGERIA AND NIGER

We eventually set off for the Algerian border at Oujda. We stopped in Algiers for a night before heading south into the Sahara, travelling on surfaced roads through Laghouat, Ghadia and on to El Golea. However, about 40 miles after leaving El Golea, the road became an un-surfaced track that had become corrugated by the extreme weather conditions. The trick was to travel at a speed of about 40 mph+, so that you travelled over the crests of the corrugations and avoided getting shaken to pieces, but that was easier said than done – particularly in an ageing diesel LR shod with Spanish remolds.

As we moved further into the Sahara the high midday temperatures made travelling unbearable, even with all the windows and air-vents open (there was no air-conditioning in vehicles back then), and so we would stop and string a tarpaulin between the LRs to create shade for everyone to rest until about 4pm when the temperature started to drop a bit. We would then drive until dusk, before stopping, making camp, eating and then bedding down at around 8.30pm. Although the daytime temperatures were unbearably high, by night it was so cold that we were glad to have our quilted sleeping bags to snuggle into. We'd be up again at dawn to hit the road and get some miles behind us before it got too hot.

My one abiding memory of the desert was going to sleep on my roof rack watching for shooting stars in the clear, un-polluted night sky and then waking at about 4am in the grey light just before the dawn with no traffic noise, no birds singing, no dogs barking - just a complete sound vacuum. That will stay with me forever. I would climb down, sit inside the LR, put a Strauss tape in the cassette player and watch the sun rise over the Sahara to the haunting sound of the Blue Danube. Pure magic.

We eventually arrived, feeling tired and battered, at In Salah - often cited as being one of the hottest spots in the world. At the time there had, reportedly, no rain for seven years - and it was beginning to feel very hot. Once you got into the desert you were required to check in at the local police station before you left a town and then register when you arrived at the next, as it wasn't difficult to become stranded without water and/or fuel if adverse conditions occurred or you wandered off-track and got lost.

The Hogar Mountains (Sahara)

Leaving In Salah we continued on corrugations before the road took us on the Hoggar route up into the Ahaggar Mountains. This was the most barren country I'd ever seen, just a rough, rock-strewn track winding between bare, weather-worn stony peaks and outcrops. It reminded me of the pictures taken of the Moon's surface – it really was a lunar landscape that made me feel as if I were travelling in another world.

Driving out of the mountains, we were surprised to come across an oasis, with palm trees and crop fields that were fed by a small stream running down from the mountains. We spotted some boys from the local settlement using sling-shots to keep birds away from their precious crops. We thought we would take the opportunity to take some water from the stream, but the boys explained that this was not good to drink, as there were goats using it further upstream. They took us to a small well that had been dug beside the stream; they lowered an old tin can several feet down the well and offered us the well water to drink. Although a little yellow, it was refreshingly cool and the sweetest water we'd tasted for a long time.

We camped the night, before driving through to Tamanrasset, an oasis city and the home city of the Tuaregs who were once the town's main inhabitants. It had originally been established as a military outpost to guard the trans-Saharan trade routes. The LRs had received a bit of a battering on the corrugations and up through the mountains; Gus had ripped the sidewall on one of his tyres, while the roof rack on my vehicle was falling apart. Gus found a new tyre at an exorbitant price while I went off, with Bill tagging along, to get my roof rack fixed. On asking around, we were directed to a stockade that housed a vehicle repair workshop. Having explained what needed doing, the

LR was assailed by several men with gas cylinders and welding torches and the work commenced, with Bill and I observing proceedings from a safe distance.

Work suddenly ceased round about midday, as a man appeared carrying a large bowl covered by a cloth. He crossed the yard and entered a lean-to at the far side of the compound. Bill and I were summoned to follow the men into the lean-to which was dimly lit by a single lightbulb hanging from the ceiling. The bowl was placed on the ground in the centre of the room and once we were all sitting round, cross-legged on the floor, the cloth was removed with a flourish to reveal a "tagine" consisting of what looked like pieces of either goat or camel intestines, with a few straggly green beans floating in a sea of oil. Pieces of flat bread were handed around and Bill and I were invited to dip in and help ourselves.

"I don't like the look of that meat," Bill whispered out of the corner of his mouth.

"Me neither," I replied.

"Let's try and avoid it and just pick out the beans," I suggested, but a few minutes later the men sitting next to us were scooping up pieces of meat insisting that we indulge ourselves, as they obviously thought we were just being polite and leaving the "best bits" for the workers. To this day, I'm pretty sure that that was the worst meal I (and probably Bill) ever had.

Work resumed after everyone had finished eating; with the work completed and the roof rack looking and feeling a lot sturdier, I was presented with the bill. It was a lot of money! I turned to Bill with a shocked expression on my face and blurted out, "Christ, they've charged us tourist rates – and I think they must have charged us for lunch as well!"

***

After a couple of days rest, having filled our jerry cans with fuel and water, we left for the border with Niger and the next stop which was Agadez – the capital city of Niger. The stretch between Tamanrasset and Agadez was about 550 miles of barren desert with no drinkable water or fuel. It was scheduled to take three to five days, depending on weather conditions. On the way to the border my LR gave a sudden lurch, so I pulled up. On inspection, I discovered that a rear spring shackle had broken – and we didn't have a spare. As the vehicle was now somewhat lopsided, we transferred most of the passengers to Gus's LR and moved as much as possible to the opposite side on mine, before slowly continuing on our way, fearing that a rear spring might suddenly burst through the floor. There were no buildings in sight when we reached the border, just a sign instructing vehicles to stop as this was the border, plus a large trough of sulphurated water fed from a hot spring bubbling up from the ground.

We sat there for a while and watched as a herd of camels arrived at the trough and drained it with loud slurping noises in a matter of minutes. Eventually a man appeared from over a hillock in a rather tatty, dusty uniform and asked us for our passports, before disappearing with them back over the hillock. While we were waiting for him to re-appear, another LR arrived carrying a French archeologist and his driver/guide. On hearing of our predicament with the LR he scrabbled around in a large box of spares they were carrying and presented us with a brand-new spring shackle, which he was happy to exchange for a bottle of Pernod (acquired duty-free in Ceuta for just such a bartering situation).

Eventually the border guard returned with our passports duly stamped. There were wheel tracks heading off in every direction, with no indication as to which direction we should take for Agadez. The guard pointed to a single tree that was visible, about a mile away and explained that we should head for the tree, then we would eventually pick up the marker posts that marked the route we needed. I heard a few years later the tree had been knocked down by a lorry! We picked up the marker posts (probably about 1km apart – although quite a few of them were missing - and continued on our way. We stopped quite late that night.

It was dark by the time we made camp and were in the process of cooking a meal when Helen suddenly whispered that someone was watching us. Gus and I dismissed it, saying she was imagining things – after all, we were in the middle of the Sahara Desert for goodness-sake. But a few minutes later she asked us to check it out – she was sure there was someone there. So, Gus and I took a torch and wandered off in the direction she'd indicated – and sure enough, about 30 metres from our camp we came across a Tuareg tribesman in his flowing indigo robes and veil, sitting on the largest camel I'd ever seen. He had approached our camp in complete silence and we had no idea how long he'd been sitting there watching us.

We invited him to come and sit with us; after he'd dismounted and hobbled his camel, we offered him tea and food. He spoke no French or English and we spoke no Arabic, but he indicated that he needed medication for his and his family's eyes. We figured that they were probably suffering from conjunctivitis caused by sand being constantly blown into their eyes, so we gave him a bottle of eye wash – one of the few things we had in plentiful supply in our first-aid kit, that we thought might be of use to him and his family. After finishing his food and tea he thanked us by placing his hands together and bowing, before remounting his camel and silently riding off into the night. Two days later we rolled into Agadez.

CENTRAL AFRICA – NORTHERN NIGERIA, CAMEROON, CHAD, RCA, AND ZAIRE

We spent a couple of days in Agadez, known as the southern gateway to the desert, recuperating from our trans-Sahara experience, even visiting the local zoo (which was very basic, although they did have a giraffe), before heading for the border with Nigeria and on to Kano, arriving on Thursday 30th March.

Sitting in a bar that evening, Gus and I got chatting to man who was the manager of a local Land Rover franchise. We decided it was a good opportunity to get the vehicles a much-needed service before setting off across the centre of the continent, so we asked if he could book us in for the next day, only to be told that the next day was Good Friday; Everything would be closed for Easter until the following Tuesday and in any case, the service bays were fully booked for another week.

While talking to us, he had been admiring the puzzle ring that Jasmine had given me the previous November in Kabul, remarking, rather pointedly, that his girlfriend would "love a ring like that!" Gus asked if there was any way we might be able to jump the queue and, with a little smile on his face as he gazed at the ring, he told us that it might be possible. Gus took me to one side and explained that I really needed to hand it over if we were going to avoid a long delay. I really didn't want to part with the ring, but Gus eventually persuaded me, pointing out that I could always get another one next time I was in Istanbul. Of course, this didn't take into account the sentimental value attached to it. I very reluctantly handed it over and we were told to present the vehicles for servicing on Tuesday morning; this would prove to be the way things tended to be done as our journey progressed through Central Africa.

Easter Sunday arrived and we'd learnt that this was the momentous day when Nigeria changed from driving on the left to driving on the right. On walking out of the campsite that morning we found that crowds were gathering on every major road junction and roundabout to watch "the action". Everyone and anyone in a uniform (including boy scouts!) had been recruited for traffic duty. Needless to say, the whole situation was chaotic. An old man came along riding his bike in all innocence, as he'd always done, on the left side of the road (no-one in his village had told him about any change). He was immediately hit with a stick by a uniformed person and instructed, much to his bemusement, but to the great amusement of the spectators, to ride on the opposite side. Needless to say, there were quite a lot of traffic accidents. Gus and I decided we would keep off the roads that day!

With our vehicles fully serviced (and minus one treasured puzzle ring) we headed east across northern Nigeria, through a narrow neck of Cameroon and on to Fort-Lamy (re-named N'Djamena a year later), which was the capital city of Chad, one of the poorest countries in the world. We made camp on the sandy banks of the Logone River for a couple of days, enjoying the luxury of swimming and bathing in fresh, clear water before moving south on a rough, unmetalled road.

A day out of Fort-Lamy my spring shackle broke again, not far from the town of Lai. We decided it would be foolish to risk driving on such a rough road with an un-shackled rear spring, so Gus headed off to check the town out, returning about three hours later with a shackle he had found in a breaker's yard on the edge of the town.

With the repairs completed, we continued south, crossing the border into the Central African Republic and on to the capital, Bangui. Having lived on catering packs of re-hydrated meals and tins of sardines since leaving Tangier, Gus suggested that we should visit a restaurant for some proper food; we soon found a reasonably respectable-looking establishment. One of the dishes on the menu was a local specialty - "pot-roast monkey", which Jim, being something of an exhibitionist, decided he was going to order. When the food arrived, Jim's dinner consisted of a miniature arm, complete with hand, fingers and fingernails – in a nice brown onion sauce. He couldn't eat it, but didn't stop talking about it as we made our way back to the LR. Bettsie had heard enough; his temper suddenly snapped and he leapt from his seat with fists flying. He was eventually restrained and Jim was somewhat subdued for the remainder of the drive back to the campsite.

After spending a couple of days in Bangui, we headed east towards Bangassou and the ferry that would take us across the Ubangui river to Zaire. We were now travelling on the edge of the tropical rainforests of Central Africa and the climate was becoming quite humid. Two days out of Bangui we came across a spectacular waterfall on the Kotto river (which was marked on the Michelin map purely as "chutes"), and decided to make camp there.

Warerfall in RCA

That afternoon a young lad came to the camp and explained in broken French and sign language that his mother had a "bad foot." He wanted us to go and look at it and maybe help her. We all piled into the LRs and drove to his village, a few kilometres down the road. On arrival a couple of stools were produced and Gus, armed with our first aid kit, sat himself down and inspected the foot which appeared to have a hole in the sole, possibly caused by leprosy. It had been stuffed with cow dung: the only "antiseptic" available to the local people.

Gus treating an infected foot in RCA

Gus proceeded to clean the infected area then dress it with penicillin powder, watched by some of the passengers, including Bill who was standing beside him. When Gus had finished, he rinsed his hands in some disinfectant and then, looking for something to dry them on, turned and wiped his hands on

Bill's shirt. Bill hadn't seen Gus rinse his hands and watched in horror as Gus wiped, what Bob thought, were leprosy-infected hands on his shirt. In a state of panic, he took off at a rate of knots towards the LRs, tearing his shirt off as he went and then throwing it into the back of one of the vehicles. I never saw him wear that shirt again despite being assured that Gus had actually rinsed his hands in disinfectant before using his shirt as a towel!

***

The next day we caught the ferry from Bangassou across the Ubangui to Zaire. There was a small customs post on the river bank with one guard in a tatty uniform, armed with an antiquated rifle. We presented our passports and were told that we would have to wait for the customs officer to return.

"Well, where is he?" we enquired.

"Over the river in Bangassou," he replied, somewhat apologetically.

"Why is he over there?"

"The beer's cheaper".

"When will he be back?"

"When his money runs out".

"When is that likely to be?"

"Don't know; might be tomorrow, or maybe the next day".

Gus had become increasingly frustrated during this conversation and in no uncertain terms, made it quite clear that we couldn't wait around for two or three days for the "bloody customs officer" to return to his post. The guard, somewhat overwhelmed by being faced with 11 irate Caucasians, finally agreed to let us into the country, but told us that we would have to report to the police in the town of Monga, about 80km down the road, in order to get our passports stamped – and we would need them stamped before we left Zaire.

Monga was an old Belgian mining town with small red-brick houses that had been built for the mine workers during the years of Belgian colonialism. We made camp on the outskirts of the town; that evening, we wandered over to a local "nightclub", comprised of a stockade with a round concrete dance floor in the centre, surrounded by a few rickety tables and chairs. There was a bar along one side of the stockade and the music "system" consisted of a 50 gallon oil drum with a record player inside it. The oil drum acted as a (very) rudimentary, but quite effective, amplifier! The local music was similar to South American samba and the couples on the dance floor were engaged in a shuffling sort of dance.

We sat at a table and after a few minutes, became aware that the dancing had stopped and there was suddenly quite a hostile atmosphere, with everyone staring at us. I should explain at this point that this area had suffered a lot of atrocities committed by Belgian mercenaries, (white, tattooed ex-military men), during the Congo's struggle for independence a few years earlier. We'd already had machetes brandished at us as we passed through villages. Gus was ex-British army and was sitting there in shorts and T-shirt, sporting tattoos on his arms and legs. Moreover, we had arrived that evening in Land Rovers (seen by locals as military vehicles). Suddenly a young lad ran across the dance floor from the bar and whispered in Gus's ear. Gus sat there nodding, and said something to the lad, who ran back to the bar and spoke to a rather large lady, obviously the owner of the establishment. She called across to the man operating the "sound system" and, as the next record started playing, she waddled out to the middle of the dance floor and was met by Gus, who then put on a classic performance, hamming it up with exaggerated wiggles and flourishes as he danced with our hostess. The atmosphere was broken, the locals all joined in on the dance floor and we ended up having a great evening sampling the local beer.

The next morning, we reported to the police station, which looked like something from an old Wild West movie, with a wooden veranda and balustrades. There we were given a severe reprimanding by the extremely officious officer in charge for having travelled into his country without having our passports officially stamped. We tried to explain the circumstances, but he was having none of it. He ordered the roof racks on both LRs to be unloaded for a customs search. There was only one way to approach this; we began unloading the roof racks - slowly, (actually it was *very* slowly, with a lot of chatting between each item), meanwhile setting up the camping stoves on the station's veranda and putting the kettles on. This had the desired effect.

"What are you doing?" demanded the officer.

"It's OK," Gus explained. "You're going to be quite some time, so we're just making a cup of tea while we wait for you to complete your search".

"No, no – you can't do that here!"

"It's OK – we're fine".

"No, no – finish; you can go. Go!"

And we did as we were bade - repacked the roof racks, got our passports stamped and went.

About 50 miles from Monga, we found ourselves on the banks of the Uele River, a tributary of the Ubangui, which we needed to cross in order to continue our journey. The ferry consisted of five wood canoes lashed together with planks across the top to form a deck which would comfortably accommodate one LR at a time. Planks were placed from the bank to the ferry and Gus drove aboard. The "crew" consisted of about half-a-dozen men who used long bamboo poles to punt the ferry to the far bank. Half way across they stopped, had a bit of a discussion between themselves and then asked for more money before they continued.

Gus: "We don't have any more money".

Another discussion ensued: "OK – give us some T-shirts".

Gus: "We only have the ones we're wearing".

Another brief discussion: "OK – give us a cigarette each".

Cigarettes were duly handed over and the first crossing was completed, followed a little later by me and my LR.

Uele River crossing in Zaire

We stopped the following afternoon to investigate on seeing a rusty Coca-Cola sign hanging on a hut in a small village. As we walked over to the hut a man came out carrying a crate of beer. He seemed pleased to see us and started chatting, explaining that he was Greek and had a coffee plantation not far from the village. He told us that government troops had stripped everything from his house, but he would welcome our company that night and we could sleep in the house, rather than putting up tents. His offer was gratefully accepted and, having stocked up with our own supply of beer, we were about to leave when a couple of New Zealanders pulled up in an old, battered VW Beetle sporting an equally-battered roof rack adorned with pots, pans and a kettle hanging from the sides. A bit more company was welcome and we all headed off to the plantation together.

We sat round a large bonfire that evening enjoying our beers and indulging in some bhang (local marijuana that the Kiwis had acquired together with a pipe to smoke it with - very powerful stuff!), while listening to our host's stories of the government harassment he'd endured and exchanging anecdotes with the two Kiwis who had bought their Beetle for $120 in Germany. It had valiantly survived the Sahara crossing and the rough, jungle tracks without missing a beat – although the shock absorbers were completely shot! We discovered later that the car had made it all the way to Uganda, but the engine had expired once they hit surfaced roads.

A few days later we arrived in the town of Isiro which had a main street consisting of a strip of tarmac with a motel at the top end owned by Yiorgos, a Greek Cypriot, who welcomed us with open arms. Gus and I were relaxing in the bar when a couple of Cypriot lads invited us to join them at their table. They told us that their fathers both owned coffee plantations about three hours' drive from the town and that they drove in at weekends for a bit of "nightlife". They asked us about ourselves and we recounted the various encounters we'd had on our trip. They seemed enthralled and suggested we move on to a bar on the outskirts of the town - where they sold ouzo! That evening, having liberally indulged ourselves of the ouzo on offer, Gus and I ended up climbing onto a table and giving an impromptu performance of the animated rugby version of Old MacDonald's farm (Gus's idea; Gus's choreography!). This went down a storm with the bar's clientele. They didn't understand a word we were singing, but loved our exaggerated prancing. We got back to the motel about 3am.

Towing a car through a pot hole in the 'road' in Zaire

It was now the beginning of the rainy season; after leaving the following morning, we were driving on a very muddy track through the jungle. It was at this point that the four-wheel drive capability of the LRs really came into its own. I was leading the way when, around mid-morning, my attention was drawn to a very dark patch on the track ahead that looked like an oil slick, possibly shed by a damaged lorry engine, and I didn't notice that the wheel ruts I had been following suddenly veered diagonally across to the opposite side of the track. Although we were only travelling about 20 mph, the LR lurched into the air and then, in slow motion, rolled gracefully on to its side – much to the amusement of Gus and his passengers who were following behind us and had a grandstand view of the whole embarrassing incident. However, no damage was done and, with all hands-on-deck, we got the LR upright again and continued on our way.

Later that afternoon we came across a Cypriot family whose car was stuck in a very large, slippery pothole filled with water. With help from some local men that appeared from nowhere out of the bush, we attached the car to my LR with a towrope and, slowly but surely managed to haul the car out and onto more manageable ground.

The Michelin maps of Africa that we were using measured, in total, two meters from top to bottom and 95 centimeters wide. In nine hours that day we travelled less than two centimeters on the map!

***

Around mid-afternoon a couple of days later, we came to a village and, noticing some chickens running around, thought it would be a bit of a treat to have some fresh meat for our meal that evening. Having located the head-man, who spoke some broken French, Gus set about bartering with him. This resulted in him acquiring two scrawny specimens which Gus quickly dispatched and plucked before handing them over to Anna and John, who were on cooking duty that day. After gaining permission from the head-man, we made camp on the outskirts of the village.

Taking a short stroll, Gus suddenly spotted a woman carrying a small child who had a large boil on his neck. He immediately went into "doctor mode", calling her over to the LR before opening up the first-aid kit, piercing the boil, squeezing the puss out, treating it with penicillin powder and applying a dressing. Word spread rapidly around the village that we were handing out FREE medical treatment. (Villagers would normally have to walk, sometimes several days, to the nearest mission and maybe pay all the money they'd been able to scrape together in a year for their treatment). Subsequently a long queue quickly formed beside the LR; Dr. Gus had a jungle clinic on his hands.

Commandeering a nearby hut as his "consultation room", Gus assigned the head-man the task of interpreting and ex-nurse Helen the role of nursing assistant, before calling his "patients" in one at a time. The head-man would explain each patient's ailment and Gus would ask Helen for the appropriate item(s) from the first-aid box. This is when our ample supply of yellow multi-vitamin tablets came into its own, Gus using it as a placebo as a last resort.

After about an hour, Gus was getting towards the end of the queue when an old man entered the hut and stood there in an old T-shirt and very baggy shorts; looking somewhat embarrassed, he nodded towards Helen and whispered something to the head-man. Realizing that this gentleman probably had a personal problem, Gus asked Helen if she could step outside while he dealt with this patient. Gus was feeling a bit overworked and frayed at the edges by this time. "OK" he demanded, "what's the problem". The old man promptly dropped his shorts and pointed to his testicles, one of which was about the size of a tennis ball! The head-man explained that the man's wife was complaining about "bad sex" and he wanted Gus to perform the same treatment that he's given to the child with the boil – pierce his testicle and squeeze it out!

"No, no – I can't do that!" Gus explained, "here" he said, quickly dipping his hand into the box of multi-vitamins and handing over two of the yellow tablets.

"Take one of these tonight and one in the morning".

The old man eagerly grasped his medication and left with a look of delight on his face.

Having "treated" half the village for various ailments, the clinic came to an end and we settled down that evening to a very welcome chicken casserole. The next morning, we awoke to find virtually the whole male population of the village lined up at the LR asking for some of our yellow tablets. We concluded that the placebo had worked far better than Gus had expected and that word had quickly spread around the village that our yellow tablets had been a great success as a placebo. It would seem that Viagra was actually discovered in Zaire in 1972, and it wasn't blue – it was yellow!

***

We were now travelling through dense jungle, stopping one afternoon to barter with a man walking along with a very large basket of mangoes which he was very happy to exchange for one of my old T-shirts. The fresh fruit was greeted with great enthusiasm and everyone ate their fill, but there was a price to pay as our stomachs weren't used to dealing with so much fresh fruit. As I drove along the next morning with all the air vents and windows open, I became aware of a very unpleasant smell and looking in my rear-view mirror I could see Bill sitting in the far corner hunched up like a little gnome, with an evil grin on his face. He'd been farting non-stop and his farts had managed to drift upwind, even in the face of the prevailing draught from the vents and open windows!

We made camp the following evening in a clearing. As we were finishing our meal the air was suddenly filled with flying termites. It seemed as if it was the ideal weather conditions for them to swarm (in the way our flying ants do on a summer's days back in the UK). As we were in the process of hurriedly clearing our things away, we noticed a group of Bambuti pygmies collecting the termites as they fell to the ground and shed their wings. We discovered later that the insects were a valuable source of fat and protein.

The next morning, as we were packing up to leave, some of the pygmies approached us, wanting to exchange their bows and arrows for sugar. The bows were made using animal gut for the string and were embroidered with monkey tails, while the arrow tips were made from pieces of tin can that had been cut to the right shape and then beaten to give them a sharp edge. I was keen to make an exchange, but Gus suggested that we could find some on the scheduled return trip, as there was no point in taking them all the way to Cape Town and back - I agreed and no exchange took place. As it transpired, we never made the return trip so I never got my pygmy bow and arrows.

A few days later the bolt holding the spring shackle in place broke again. I managed to make it to the town of Mambasa and find a small workshop that was able to turn a new bolt for us on their lathe. However, being as it was un-tempered mild steel, it didn't last long before shearing through. Fortunately, just a few miles on, we came to a small garage sporting a single hand-operated petrol pump – you turned a handle to draw five litres up into a glass chamber mounted on top of the pump and then a tap on the nozzle of a connecting hose was opened to empty the contents into the fuel tank. The owner was a Pakistani gentleman. We asked, without much hope, whether he might possibly have a shackle somewhere. He disappeared out the back and eventually returned carrying, a brand new and complete shackle, much to our surprise and delight. Then came the bartering. We were eventually able to buy it at an exorbitant price - plus a bottle of Johnnie Walker, another of our Ceuta acquisitions. A couple of days later, we crossed the border into Uganda.

EAST AFRICA – UGANDA, KENYA AND TANZANIA

We crossed the equator on our first day in Uganda and made camp early afternoon beside Lake Edward in the Queen Elizabeth National Park. Taking a walk along the lake shore, Gus and I came across the stinking remains of a dead hippo, half in and half out of the water. It was being attacked by a shoal of ravenous catfish. I'd acquired of couple of hand fishing lines for our trip and so, cutting some pieces from the carcass and baiting our hooks, we attempted to catch ourselves a fish, but to no avail. However, on our way back to camp we came across an overspill pond and on casting our lines on the off-chance that it may hold some fish, we ended up with two specimens, each weighing around the one kilo mark. We presented them to the passengers on our return. Using his bush-craft skills, Bettsie filleted them and fried them up for that evening's meal, which seemed to go down very well – except Gus and I didn't really fancy any, as we knew what we'd been using for bait!

We re-crossed the equator, heading north the next day to Fort Portal. When we arrived, we were told that we had been very lucky to get away unscathed the previous night, as there were a lot of lions in and around the area where we'd been camping. However, on the up-side, we found a general store in the town that sold Cadbury's chocolate - happy passengers!

We made camp at the municipal campsite on the outskirts of the town, which was very basic and had no bar. So, that evening, having recruited a local man to guide us to a local hostelry, we all piled into Gus's LR. It was pitch dark and raining, and our guide suggested, rather than take a circuitous route to town, we should take a short—cut across a field. We took his advice, and were surprised to encounter a pole with a flag on it half way across, before eventually arriving at our destination. Next morning, as we were driving alongside the local golf course, we observed a group of elderly men involved in an animated conversation while pointing towards a set of deep wheel ruts running right across the middle of the 18th green. We pretended not to notice and continued on our way north towards the Murchison Falls National Park.

The green, rolling hills of Western Uganda reminded me of Devon – but with elephants; we would drive over a rise and there would be the stunning sight of a herd of maybe 100 or more spread out on the slopes below us. Murchison Falls was just spectacular. I spent a day fishing the Victoria Nile below the falls for Nile perch using a rudimentary rod and lure hired from the park lodge at the campsite, but with no success. After a couple of days resting up and relaxing, we moved on to Kampala, the capital city of Uganda, and we were all delighted to discover an excellent Indian restaurant the first night there – sheer luxury!

"Goes without saying!" (Trans-Africa - Uganda)

We headed east from Kampala to Jinja, crossing at the Owen Falls, the source of the Nile where it flows out of Lake Victoria. Progress was quite rapid now, as we were travelling on surfaced roads and were soon crossing the border into Kenya. Another day driving down the Rift Valley took us to Lake Nakuru, where a stunning sight greeted us; the perimeter of the lake was hardly discernible due to the continually shifting mass of pink flamingos, with thousands upon thousands of the birds feeding on algae in the warm alkaline waters – truly one of nature's wonders.

Another 100km and we arrived in Nairobi, parked up and headed straight to Poste Restante, with everyone eager to collect correspondence from parents and loved-ones. On returning to the LRs we discovered that both vehicles had been broken into (too easily done on the LRs), with cameras and personal effects stolen, including my pair of camel-hide boots that I'd had made-to-measure during my last stop in Kabul. Gus went off in a rage to find the individual who we had paid to guard the car-park, pinning him against the wall and shaking him violently, but it wasn't going to get our stolen belongings back.

The police weren't really interested; we were later told that this was a well organised racket, with spotters out on the main roads approaching Nairobi watching for foreign vehicles, particularly LRs, knowing that the first stop for most of them would be the car-park beside Poste Restante and that the occupants would be away from their vehicle for some time while they collected their mail. The "guard" on the car-park was obviously in the pay of the thieves.

We telexed Frontier advising them that we had arrived in Nairobi and requesting a top-up to our trip funds for the remainder of our journey to Cape Town. The reply which came 24 hours later, stunned everyone. It said that, as the trip had taken an unexpectedly long time to reach Nairobi, and had been more costly than had been calculated, and not enough passengers had booked to warrant a return trip from Cape Town to London, we were to terminate the trip there and then. The passengers would be offered a flight to Cape Town or back to London. Gus would fly straight back to London the following day, while I was to stay on to organise the passengers' on-going journey and garage the LRs before flying back to the UK.

I decided that we would take a week out to travel to the north of Tanzania while the on-going travel arrangements were being organised back in Crawley. All but Bettsie and Tricksy had opted to fly on to Cape Town, while the two Aussies had decided o fly back to London with me. The passengers were not happy. They had split into two groups, seven of them becoming resentful, seeing me as Frontier's representative, while Bettsie and Tricksy realised that I was trying to make the best of a bad situation and remained supportive.

We headed south from Nairobi, driving through a corner of the Amboseli game reserve before crossing into Tanzania and on to Arusha. Each time we stopped we encountered Maasai tribespeople, famous for their fearsome reputation as warriors and cattle-rustlers. The Maasai warriors are perfect examples of dedicated male grooming, spending years tending to and caring for their intricately styled hair, using ashes, clay, animal fats and ochre to style and colour the hair, which is formed into thinly braided strands and woven together with cotton or wool threads. They are the only group permitted to wear their hair long (Maasai women shave their heads). They look stunning with their colourful beaded earrings, necklaces and red robes. The warriors' "manes" symbolize the African lion's strength and masculine beauty.

Over the next few days, we travelled east to the Ngorongoro Crater, the world's largest inactive, intact and unfilled volcanic caldera. It is part of the Ngorongoro Conservation Area which is considered to be the seat of humanity after the discovery of the earliest known specimens of the human genus there. Back in 1972, the crater was one of the most-dense known populations of wild animals, including black rhinos. Before leaving Ngorongoro, the two Aussies and I bought a kilo of steak from the local village butcher for 7.5 Tanzanian shillings (about 38p) which we demolished with great relish that evening. We moved on to the sweeping plains of the Serengeti, seeing many gazelles, zebra, wildebeest, lions and one leopard.

Stopping in Arusha on our way back to Nairobi, I was fascinated by beautiful, intricately carved ebony sculptures created by the Makonde people, many of which represented demons and spirits that had allegedly been seen in the forests (possibly under the hallucinogenic influence of bhang). Unfortunately, I had no money left to buy any of these pieces at the time. However, years later I acquired a number of pieces including one stunning, large and very heavy example that I found on eBay and had shipped from Australia - the shipping cost was more than the actual price of the sculpture!

A few days after our return to Nairobi, Bettsie, Tricksy and I bade goodbye to the rest of the group and awaited details of our flights to London. I had run out of funds and was being supported by the two Aussies. I would telex back to Crawley every couple of days asking for money to be sent, but I would get the same old message back: "Have sent money. Don't know what's happening. Will chase Amex and send again. Cheers – Pat)." One morning, the three of us were sitting in the Thorn Tree, a popular gathering place in the centre of the city. The two Aussies were telling me about a stopover in Hong Kong on their trip from Australia to the UK. They had met a Nigerian guy there who was selling carpets that he'd bought in Afghanistan, explaining to them that he was then going to use the money he made to buy watches and transistor radios to take back and sell in Afghanistan. It could only be one person.

"Was his name Abdul – and did he say no sweat a lot?"

"Ah, yeah – shit, that was him – Abdul No-Sweat"!

The world was proving to be a very small place indeed.

***

One evening the boys suggested we should have a night out. We headed for the "Starlight Club" in the centre of town, where a blonde Japanese lady was performing an erotic dance which involved quite a large python. Towards the end of the evening, we were approached by three "hostesses" who sat themselves down at our table and started chatting. I left a little later with one of the girls, Suzanne, while the two Aussies headed back to the campsite. I ended up living with Suzanne for the next few weeks while I waited for Frontier to arrange a flight for us back to London. Suzanne shared a large house in a well-to-do area near the racecourse with about six other ladies-of-the-night who I would provide a taxi service for using the Land Rover, dropping them off at various clubs and bars around the city each night.

They took it in turns to cook a communal meal each day, providing me with huge, heaped plates of food while telling me, "You are too thin, and cannot go home to your mother like that!" Suzanne would occasionally give me money so that I could take her for a meal at a little local restaurant that did an excellent fillet steak with a black pepper sauce. No money was forthcoming from Frontier despite all the telex messages, but the girls would give me money to buy fuel for the LR, so that I could continue providing them with transport.

Suzanne was Kikuyu and asked me one day if I could drive her to see her parents who lived and worked in a village on a coffee plantation about three hours' drive from the city. We arrived that afternoon and, as we walked from the LR to her parents hut, I was pelted with stones by some of the local boys. I realized later that the Kikuyu were one of the dominant tribes involved in the Mau Mau uprising against the British in the 1950s and, at least out in the provinces, a white man was still considered to be "the enemy". Suzanne's parents spoke no English and it was obvious that my presence made them uncomfortable, so after she had given them some money and talked to them for about 30 minutes, we returned to Nairobi.

Bettsie and Tricksy were still living at the municipal campsite and we'd meet up most days at the Thorn Tree club, which is where I met Seychelles Joe. He was a small, cheerful man from – yes - the Seychelles. He was also a friend of Suzanne's. I was sitting with Joe one morning when he asked if I could drive him over to Little Harlem, a shanty town on the outskirts of the city, as he had something bulky to collect there. When we arrived, Joe told me to park up opposite a church in the centre of the town and wait for him there. After about ten minutes he returned carrying a large sack which he dumped in the back of the LR and I drove him back to town. I was taken aback the next day to find a report in the Daily Nation on how the police had been cracking down on Little Harlem, it being the centre of the marijuana trade in Nairobi. The centre-page spread sported a large photo of the church I had been parked outside and it suddenly dawned on me what I'd been transporting for Joe the previous day – a large sack of bhang!

We flew out of Nairobi on the 8th June, exactly a month after I had arrived in Kenya, returning to London via Cairo on a United Arab Airways charter flight, having spent the month stranded in Nairobi with no money. Frontier had paid just £45 each for our tickets.

12. THE SUMMER OF '72

Arriving back in England in June, the three of us headed for my sister Margaret's place in Ilford and spent the evening with her and her Irish partner, Mick "the diver" (he was a navy-trained deep-sea diver). We unwound from our journey at their favourite drinking club, where we ruffled Mick's feathers somewhat by setting out to, and succeeding in drinking him and his mates under the table. Leaving the club in the early hours of the morning, Mick (who had obviously had his feathers ruffled by us) announced that we couldn't stay at his place. So, leaving him at the side of the road to find his own way home, Margaret drove us the ten miles to my parents' place in Brentwood arriving on their doorstep at 3.00am. My father eventually answered the door in his pyjamas and dressing gown.

"Sorry Dad – just got back from Africa. Is it OK for me and my mates to stay the night?"

Looking bemused and not too happy about being woken up in the middle of the night, he muttered, "Well you'll have to sort yourselves out with sleeping arrangements," and took himself straight off back to bed. We promptly chucked our sleeping bags on the lounge floor and bedded down for what was left of the night.

As soon as I was up the following morning, I rang Frontier and spoke to Colin Payten. Realising that I wasn't at all happy with the situation I'd been left in in Nairobi and the way I'd been treated, and not wanting to lose me, now one of his most experienced drivers, he took a very placatory stance and asked what I'd like to do for the rest of the summer.

In 1972 Frontier had started operating "air-trips", basing drivers with fully-equipped vehicles in Morocco and Greece and then flying groups in and out by charter flight for two and three-week tours; one group would fly out as the next flew in.

Without hesitation I replied, "I want to do Greek air-trips".

"Fine, no problem. Get down to Crawley by this evening. You can stay at my place tonight and I'll fly you over to Bruges in the morning. We'll sort you out a Transit and you can head off down to Greece".

I should explain that Colin held a pilot's licence and had a little Piper Cherokee aircraft parked at Gatwick. Explaining the situation to my two Aussie mates, I left them in the safe hands of my mother and headed to Crawley. Early next morning I was air-borne, flying in to Lac Lopam to collect a fully-equipped Transit. A few days later I arrived at Camping Nea Kiffissia, where I'd be based for the remainder of the summer season.

Frontier's air-trip programme opened up a completely new part of Greece for me. With passengers arriving at Athens airport on charter flights, the groups would spend three or four nights in Athens, based at Camping Nea Kiffissia, before heading south to the Peloponnese, across the spectacular Corinth Canal which connects the Gulf of Corinth in the <u>Ionian Sea</u> with the <u>Saronic Gulf</u> in the <u>Aegean Sea</u>. Cutting through the narrow <u>Isthmus of Corinth</u>, the rock walls rise 90 metres (300 ft) above sea level at a near-vertical 80° angle. It separates the <u>Peloponnese</u> from the <u>Greek</u> mainland, the canal arguably makes the peninsula an <u>island</u>. We would visit ancient Corinth, walking in the footsteps of St Paul, before travelling past Nemea where Hercules slayed the Nemean lion by strangling it with his bare hands. Then we would move on to the archaeological site of Mycenae - a relic of past glories stretching back some 4,000 years. This is the place from which Agamemnon set out for Troy. Then we passed through Argos, one of the <u>oldest continuously inhabited cities</u> in the world, and the oldest in Europe, and ancient Tiryns where Hercules was given his 12 tasks by King Eurystheus, before driving to Nafplio, the first modern capital of Greece (from 1827 to 1834 following the War of Independence), eventually arriving in the picturesque village of Tolo.

***

Tolo as an area of land had been given to 5 families from Crete who had been banished by the island's new ruler, Egyptian Viceroy Mohammed Ali Pasha. He had been given the island by the Ottomans in 1821 as reward for his services to them. Following the War of Independence, in 1834, a "city" was founded by Royal Decree at the Port of Tolo and named Minoa in honour of Minos, the great king of ancient Crete. The land was divided between the five Cretan families who first settled in the area and the village eventually became known as Tolo from 1916. To this day the land is still essentially divided between the original five families, although they have inter-married over the years with families from the surrounding villages such as Asini and Drepano. However, the culture of the village is still very much Cretan.

Tolo was essentially a fishing village situated about 10km from Nafplio, but by the late '60s with its golden sands, gently sloping beach, crystal-clear water and small off-shore islands it was beginning to attract tourists who could find accommodation in the few small hotels. These were mainly used by visiting Greeks - predominantly Athenians. There were also three small campsites on the outskirts of the village – Camping Swiss, Camping Lido and Camping Asteria (Stars) for the increasing number of young foreign tourists. Although most of the overland groups stayed at Camping Lido, I opted for Camping Stars, as they had a small hotel behind the campsite where they would give me a free room if they had one spare when I arrived. I would be greeted each time with a big gold-toothed smile, kisses and a bear hug from the site manager, Aphrodite.

The village consisted of one main street running parallel to the beach, that terminated at the harbour. In the centre of the village was Taverna Paradisos, which was run by twin brothers in their early twenties, Stavros and Vasilis, and their mother Katerina, who had been widowed when the boys were eight years old. The taverna consisted of a small one-storey building on the main street that housed the kitchen and the fridges containing beers, wines and soft drinks, while all the tables were at the back of the building, stretching all the way down to the beach, laid out under the shade of large, mature eucalyptus trees. I came to know many of the locals as friends during my regular visits. These included Aphrodite (who was the brothers' aunt), Yiannis (who owned a small open-air disco), Stavros and Vasilis and their niece Marika (a Greek junior javelin champion who was keen to learn English), her younger brother Dimitris, who developed into an excellent bouzouki player under Stavros's tuition, and their cousin Vangelis who became a virtuoso on the guitar and eventually took over the family taverna, To Steki, situated on the beach.

The bay of Tolo had several off-shore islands which created a natural harbour. The sea was flat-calm and crystal-clear, with many small, colourful fishing boats moored in the harbour and just off shore. On the far side of the bay was a mountain range running down the spine of the Argolida peninsula, forming the backdrop to a stunning view. It all made for the most wonderful place in which to enjoy the hospitality, food and wine on offer at Paradisos.

The food, cooked by Katerina, was good, traditional taverna fare and ridiculously cheap (a group of 12 could eat and drink for under £10, while I always ate and drank free of charge). I bonded with the twins straight away, enjoying and sometimes falling victim to their wicked sense of humour. In common with most tavernas back then, Paradisos boasted a jukebox that carried both current British/American pop and traditional Greek music; we would witness spontaneous Greek dancing virtually every night. Stavros was an excellent bouzouki player, often taking his bouzouki to play and sing traditional songs late into the evening. To sit there at a table laden with good food and wine, listening to the gentle lapping of the sea and beautiful bouzouki music was my idea of paradise. I instantly fell in love with the village and, in the years to come, Tolo became my second home.

Leaving Tolo we would travel across the centre of the Peloponnese to Olympia and the stadium where the Olympic Games began, before heading north, boarding the ferry at Aiyion, crossing the Gulf of Corinth to Itea and driving up to Delphi, on the lower southern slopes of Mount Parnassus. The Oracle of Delphi, the Pythia, was a priestess who would prophesy from the tripod in the sunken adyton of the Temple of Apollo. The god himself was believed to speak through this Oracle. When asked a question, the Oracle never gave a direct answer, but spoke in riddles. It was then up to the inquiring party as to how to interpret them.

The itinerary then took us up the west coast to Igoumenitsa, where we would catch the ferry to Corfu, spending three or four days there before returning to the mainland and driving up through the Pindus mountains and on to the stunning spectacle of Meteora and it's monastaries, before heading on for a couple of days on the beach at Platamon and then back to Athens.

I would wave goodbye to one group of passengers as they went off to board the plane that the next group had just arrived on. A couple of hours later I was back in Camping Nea Kifissia and briefing my new group.

***

By early October the last group had left and I was due to drive the Transit back to the UK. Chris Kessler, Frontier's bookings administrator had flown down for a short break and she was to accompany me back to the UK. Chris had made friends with a couple of Canadian girls on the campsite who were making

165

their way to the UK so, as we had an empty Transit, we offered them a lift which they gladly accepted.

A couple of days before leaving we went for souvlakis and some cheap wine at a local grill bar. The evenings were beginning to get quite a bit cooler and on returning to the campsite I decided to have an early night, as I was starting to shiver. That night I began to sweat, then fell into a fever and became delirious. I can remember having a long, rambling conversation about football with my father (who obviously wasn't there) and eventually woke mid-morning feeling completely drained. The following day I felt fine, but became feverish and delirious again that evening. I realised that I hadn't continued to take my anti-malaria pills for the couple of weeks required following my return from Africa, and this was the consequence.

We set off the following day, my intention being to drive all that day, through the night and the next day, up to the Yugoslav border, straight through Yugoslavia and on to Austria, before stopping for a night and then continuing straight through to the ferry at Zeebrugge. I had a malaria attack that night while driving through Yugoslavia and another two nights later driving through Brussels at 5am, with a sleeping bag wrapped round my shoulders. I was sweating, shaking and gripping the steering wheel, while cursing the Belgians for having changed the Brussels road system since my trip down and the three girls for being asleep in the back of the bus. Needless to say, I missed the early ferry and headed for the campsite at Lac Loppem to wait for the late afternoon sailing.

I arrived at my parents' house late that evening. My mother took one look at me exclaiming, "Good lord – what's the matter with you?" Although she hadn't seen me for four months, she realised straight away that all was not well. The next morning I went to my local doctor, who took a blood sample and then rang me back in the afternoon to confirm that I had malaria. He instructed me to report to the local hospital. They put me in a bed, requested medication to be sent from Manchester (the hospital had never had a case of malaria before), and I was cured within 24 hours, although they kept me in for a few more days under observation. Apparently, I had the non-recurring strain of malaria and thankfully I've not had an attack since. Having been discharged from hospital with a clean bill of health and having regained my strength, I travelled down to Crawley, only to discover that Frontier had "run out of money", (they were basically bankrupt), owing me one month's wages.

A footnote:- on about the second day after my recovery in hospital I was told that they held their monthly forum for local GPs to discuss unusual cases. As they had never had a case of malaria, they asked if I was willing to participate, which of course I was. They wheeled me in and having explained my situation, opened the floor to questions. The one indelible memory I have of that session was when one GP (presumably an intelligent gentleman) asked if I could remember being bitten!

"Well," I replied, "I was bitten by a lot of mosquitos during my trip through Africa – but I can't remember which one actually gave me malaria".

13. AN EVENTFUL CHRISTMAS

F eeling somewhat aggrieved regarding my lost wages, I headed for Brighton and immediately gained employment with Dave Latchford, servicing and driving his vans and minibuses for the winter. After a couple of weeks sleeping on peoples' floors and sofas, I had enough money to rent a bedsit close to Brighton station.

Christmas was soon upon us and Dave lent me one of his minibuses to travel up to Ilford on Christmas Eve to spend the festive season with my sister Mags, who told me on arrival that I'd had a phone call from a lady by the name of Jasmine who wanted me to contact her.

James Taylor and the words of "Fire and Rain" came rushing back to me – *"but I always thought that I'd see you again"*. It was 13 months since I had I left her in Kabul, now it was happening.

I was overjoyed and rang her straight away. She had been staying for a few days with some people in Hammersmith. When she heard my voice, she began to cry.

"Can you come and collect me?"

"Of course!" I replied, "I'll be there in about an hour".

I checked with Mags that it would OK for Jasmine to join us for Christmas, before driving the 20 miles to Hammersmith in double-quick time. Jasmine met me at the door and flung her arms round me. Pulling me close and kissing me she invited me in to wait while she collected her things. There was a group of hippies sitting and lying about, passing a couple of joints around and I was invited to join them.

"Be careful," Jasmine warned me, "that's Lebanese black and it's really strong!"

I should have taken heed. I ended up very stoned, and it took me two hours to drive the 26 miles back to Ilford at a snail's pace.

***

Christmas Day dawned; having Jasmine by my side was the best present I could have wished for. We sat down for one of Mags' sumptuous Christmas dinners (my sister was a great cook), together with Mags' partner Mick and Frank, his best friend from British navy days. It was a happy gathering; Jasmine, who was quite a shy young lady sat there quietly enjoying the good-humoured banter between Mick and Frank. After the meal, having eaten and drunk far too much, we all retired to the sofa where the conversation continued. Jasmine was sitting quietly next to Frank when he suddenly turned to her.

"Mick tells me you read palms," and holding out his hand while chuckling away "Come on read this".

She really didn't want to, but Frank was very insistent, "No, come on - give me a reading, give me a reading".

Eventually; somewhat reluctantly, she started to read his palm. Frank wasn't really listening and was still chatting away to Mick, when Jasmine, after studying part of his hand quite intently for a while, suddenly announced, "Someone you're closely connected to has recently had an abortion". Frank literally leapt a foot off the sofa, started shaking and became very angry.

"How do you know that? You have no right to know that! Only two people in the world know that! Right, come on; tell me some more, tell me some more!"

Jasmine just shrank away and refused to continue. Needless to say, the mood was somewhat subdued for the rest of the afternoon and evening. That night as we lay in bed, Jasmine was still upset. As I held her and tried to comfort her, I asked how she had discovered this information from his hand. She started crying softly, eventually explaining that she had had an abortion a few months earlier and afterwards had noticed that she had a new line on the side of her hand. She paused, took a deep breath and then told me, "He had the same line".

We spent another couple of days in Ilford before Jasmine accompanied me back to Brighton and my insalubrious basement bedsit. The situation we found ourselves in really wasn't the best one for our relationship to blossom. I was going off to work for Dave each day and taking the occasional evening driving job, while Jasmine, knowing no-one in Brighton and, being a shy person, just sat in the bedsit all day reading and waiting for me to return, becoming more and more depressed. Having been raised in "white" South Africa, she had no domestic skills, so I had to prepare and cook our meals every evening on my return. One evening, she asked if she could help with anything and I suggested that she might want to wash the potatoes while I prepared the rest of the meal. When I went over to the sink where she seemed to be taking rather a long time, I found her scrubbing the potatoes very thoroughly in a bowl of soapy water. It was only after chastising her and consequently upsetting her (unforgivably), that I realised that she had never been involved or schooled in kitchen practises. That evening, I explained that I wasn't able to look after her properly in my current situation and that she needed to learn to be more independent. Jasmine sadly left the next morning and eventually joined her father who was living in an ashram, somewhere in Buckinghamshire. I only heard from her one more time, when she sent me a "prospectus" for the ashram, explaining it's ideology and asking me to send her a cloak that she had left at my bedsit.

14. A GREEK SUMMER

I worked for Dave through the winter and into the spring, while keeping in touch with Bettsie, who had decided to stay on in London, rather than return to Oz with Tricksy, and had been working as a labourer on building sites.

Having become disillusioned with Frontier I decided I'd like to do a "Roy Williams" and spend the summer relaxing in Greece. When I next spoke to Bettsie he said, "I'm up for that if you want some company". A few weeks later we got together in Brighton and worked out a plan of action over a few beers - as you do. Having totted up the money we'd both saved over the winter, we decided to attend the local car auction at Shoreham, buy a vehicle and then head off to Greece. Later that week we were the proud owners of an ex- GPO, olive green Ford Anglia Van, acquired for the princely sum of £65.

So, early in May, after giving our van a thorough check over, servicing and oil change, and with £100 in our kitty, we threw a couple of sleeping bags and a tent in the back and set off for our summer in Greece. I had kept in touch with Dimitris after he'd left Brighton and gone back to work for his father in Istanbul. When he heard that I was heading down to Greece with an Aussie friend he suggested that we make a bit of a detour and stay with his family for a few days at their summer house outside

Istanbul. Our stay with the family was a welcome luxury after the long drive down. We were treated like kings, with some wonderful meals of local blue crabs, grilled fish and meats, together with beautiful salads and various vegetable dishes.

We had a couple of glorious days relaxing, eating and drinking with Dimitris and his parents before saying our goodbyes and crossing back into Greece. The last time I had spoken with Roy Williams, he had told me that Theo, the owner of the taverna in Heraclizia village square, had moved from the village and had set up a beach taverna in Nea Kavali, just east of Kavalla, so I thought we should drop in to see him on our way through to Heraclizia. Theo greeted me like a long-lost friend, with a huge bear hug and kisses on each cheek, before ushering us to sit at a table which was rapidly loaded with food and various beverages.

Having eaten our fill, we erected our tent next to the taverna and spent the afternoon swimming and just relaxing on the beach with a beer or two, before wandering back into the taverna that evening. It wasn't long before dishes of delicious food began to appear from the kitchen and fill the table in front of us. It was a grand evening eating, drinking and watching some of the local lads dancing to traditional music from the juke box. We slept well that night.

Waking early next morning, with the heat of sun making it impossible for anything resembling a lie-in, we were treated to a breakfast of fried eggs swimming in a sea of green olive oil and chips, before being invited to go out fishing for mackerel with one of the local fishermen. After returning from a not very successful morning's fishing with just a couple of small fish, we were greeted by Theo and ushered to a table which was, again, soon laden with food and drink. I sat there as we finished our lunch feeling blissfully contented and thinking "This is why I wanted to spend the summer here in Greece," when Bettsie turned to me with a troubled look on his face.

"I'm a bit worried mate".

"About what?"

"Well – you know we have only a limited amount of money to last us for the summer.

"Yeah?"

"Well, I'm worried about how much all this food and booze is going to cost us".

"I don't think it's going to cost us anything".

"What d'yer mean?"

"Well Theo considers me to be an old friend and this is Greek hospitality – it's on him".

"No, no mate. I'm an outback Aussie and I was bought up to always pay my way!"

And with that he got up from the table, went across to Theo and thrust a 500 drachma note in his hand. Theo looked at it and came over to me with a puzzled look on his face.

"What's this?" he asked.

I shrugged. "He wants to pay for all the food and drink that we've had".

He looked at the money in his hand, looked at Bettsie, looked back at me, did a double take and then screwed up the banknote, spat on it, threw it on the floor and stalked off into the kitchen. Bettsie looked at me.

"What did he do that for?"

"Look mate, this is Greece and, as I said, this is Greek hospitality. He's provided all this because I'm a friend. He's done this because he wants to, not because he feels he has to. If I'm happy, he's happy. That's the way Greeks are – it's the way in which they approach life in general".

"Yeah, fair dos mate – but he doesn't know me".

"No, but you're a friend of mine, so that makes you a friend of his! You've insulted him by trying to pay for his hospitality".

We sat down that evening and ordered food and drinks, which were plonked without ceremony on the table by Theo who then disappeared back into the kitchen. As soon as we'd finished a bill for the meal was slapped on the table. I looked at Bettsie and remarked, "I think you've broken the spell, mate!"

***

We left Theo's beach a couple of days later and travelled down to Athens, arriving at Camping Nea Kifissia, where I was welcomed with open arms by Komianidis. I explained to George that I was not driving overland this year, but that Bettsie and I had decided to spend the summer in Greece.

He smiled. "Not a problem. You stay on the campsite as long as you like. You take whatever food you want from the restaurant kitchen. You pay nothing. The only thing you pay for is your drink!"

We spent a leisurely couple of months living on the campsite and enjoying the evening entertainment at the restaurant/nightclub, where I became good friends with a some of the local regulars and one of the resident band, a Libyan saxophone player and a bit of a charmer - with a lot of stamina!. He would often disappear for up to three times in a single night, each time with a different woman on the back of his motorbike, for about 20 minutes in between performances (apparently for another type of performance).

About three weeks into our stay, I was offered a job by one of my new friends at his brother's printing business in an Athens basement below a bakery. I would travel in each morning and help by loading paper into one of the printers (hot work), before being sent to get a fresh loaf from the bakery and some olives and feta from the local grocers for our lunch. I wasn't very good at loading the paper and although the work was helping out with our finances, I felt I was taking money under false pretences and "resigned" after about three weeks.

We'd been on the campsite for a couple of months when we met up with two Australian girls who arrived on the site in a Volkswagen estate car that they'd bought in Germany, before travelling down through Europe. I got chatting to them and they asked if I knew of a typical fishing village where they could spend a few days swimming and relaxing.

"As a matter-of-fact I do – a perfect little place called Tolo! It's about a three-hour drive, but well worth it; a beach taverna, little off-shore islands and perfect crystal-clear water for swimming. We can come down with you if you like to show you the way and introduce you to some of the friends I have in the village".

So off we went to spend some welcome time in Tolo enjoying the hospitality of Stavros and Vassilis at Paradisos. We returned four days later to find Bill Buchanan waiting for us. I had met and made friends with Bill the previous year when he had been working as a driver for Hughes Overland, but was now the operations manager for Minitrek Overland. He had heard Bettsie and I were in Athens and had flown down from London to find us. Minitrek had several drivers based at the campsite with fully-equipped Transits, running air-trips round Greece. However, the company had been getting some seriously negative reports about two of the drivers and wanted to replace them, on Bill's recommendation, with Bettsie and me. We duly accepted Bill's offer of work for the remainder of the season.

The Minitrek Experience.

I was to run my trips in convoy with Gary Fisher who I'd met a few times on the campsite, although he wasn't someone I had really struck up any kind of friendship with. Bettsie was to run his trips in convoy with another driver, one week in advance of ours and we were thus gainfully employed for the next two and a half months until the end of the season.

I came to think of Gary as one of life's victims; he was intelligent and well educated, but he had a naivety about him and seemed to have a problem coping with life's little intricacies, which I found rather endearing. He became a constant source of amusement for me and made me laugh a lot, getting quite perplexed and scratching his head about some of the odd situations in which he found himself.

On our first trip I introduced Gary to the benefits of using Camping Stars in Tolo where we were given a twin room in their hotel to share. I woke about 08.30 the first morning to see Gary sitting out on the balcony in his dressing gown, peering down at his lap.

"Morning Gary".

"Oh – good morning," he replied as he got up, wandered over to me and sat down beside my bed.

"Look – I've found this on my balls. What is it?"

I looked. "Wo - that's crabs!"

"Oh no – is it?" He began to panic. "What am I going to do about it?"

"Come on, get dressed and we'll go down and see Stav and Vasilis – they'll know what to do".

Ten minutes later we were standing in Paradisos with the two brothers while I explained Gary's predicament, where upon they erupted in fits of laughter.

"Munopsolis! Ella Katerina!" Stavros shouted to his mother, who was busy in the kitchen, *"Gary eki munopsolis!"* ("Gary has crabs!") Katerina looked up, and with a little toss of the head and an unconcerned tut remarked, *"Entaksi – den pirazi"* ("OK - never mind"), and carried on with her cooking.

Vasiis grabbed a tin of fly spray off a shelf and, with a wicked chuckle, offered it to Gary. "Here use this – it will get rid of them". I winced, but said nothing.

Gary took it, looked at Vasilis and asked, "Will that be OK?"

"Yeah – no problem," came the reply (delivered with another chuckle).

With that Gary pulled the front of his shorts out and gave his family jewels a blast of fly spray. Silence. The brothers and I looked at each other - and then an agonised scream rent the air as Gary started hopping around the room clutching his crotch, causing the brothers to collapse with uncontrolled mirth before Vasilis took him outside, got him to strip off, hosed him down and then went off to the village pharmacy to get the correct medication for him.

***

The summer continued with a scheduled trip every fortnight. Towards the end of September, we met our penultimate groups of passengers from the plane and drove them back to Nea Kiffissia to settle them in and give them the usual briefing for their forthcoming trip. As our new passengers sat in the restaurant that evening relaxing after their flight, my attention was drawn to a very attractive young lady in Gary's group. I wandered over, sat down opposite her, leaned across the table and came out with what I thought was the classic chat-up line at the time. "What's a nice girl like you doing in a place like this?" which seemed to be received reasonably well. I discovered that her name was Christine and she was living in Brighton having completed a teacher training course there. We spent a very pleasant evening chatting about Brighton and the forthcoming trip, before retiring to our respective tents.

Two days into the trip, we were at the Hobby Disco – a small open-air establishment on the outskirts of Tolo, drinking Metaxa and gassoza (five drachma for a large glass), and dancing the night away. I waited for a slow, romantic number to hit the turntable, wandered over to Chris and invited her to join me on the dance floor, where we were soon smooching in a close embrace. Getting positive vibes back from my advances, I whispered, "Your tent, or mine?" which resulted in us spending the night together.

Having "poached" Chris from Gary's group, she and I spent the rest of the trip sharing a tent together. As we kissed goodbye at the airport at the conclusion of her 'holiday romance', I asked Chris for her phone number and address in Brighton, noting that she hadn't bothered asking me for my contact details, and suggested she look up Gus when she got home, as he was working, temporarily at that time, as a chef at the Temple Bar pub in Brighton.

The last two groups of the year arrived a couple of hours later, on the plane that Chris and her fellow group members would be travelling back on. As we would be taking the Transits back to the UK following this final trip, the groups would be returning overland with us, thus saving Minitrek the return airfare for them. However, before we left Athens, we were informed that Minitrek had "gone bust" – which was annoying, as (yet again) I was owed a month's wages. It was suggested that I should forget about the return trip and sell the minibus, but I decided that it would be wrong to leave my 12 passengers stranded in Athens so, following one final circuit of the Peloponnese, Gary and I headed north in convoy to the Yugoslav border and the trek back through Europe.

Methoni beach 1973, with fellow driver Francis

15. A NEW CHALLENGE, FATE AND A RESCUE MISSION

I arrived at Minitrek's office in Kingston-upon-Thames in late October, reluctantly relinquished my minibus and asked whether my outstanding wages would be forthcoming, only to be told that the receivers had been called in and they would "look into it". A couple of other drivers were there asking the same question; they offered me a sofa until I got myself sorted out and mentioning that they and several others had been taken on as drivers by Minster Cars based just outside Kingston in Thames Ditton, a new start-up providing mini-cab and chauffeur hire services.

I was taken the next day to meet Trevor, the young owner, and his wife Elaine, to see if he wanted another reliable driver. He looked at me with a pained expression as I stood there – afro hair, scruffy beard,Tshirt, pink corduroy jeans and sandals. He explained that I would really have to get a haircut and shave my beard before he could even consider employing me, as all his drivers were smart and clean-shaven. They all wore the company "uniform" of a three-piece, tailor-made suit. He gave me an apologetic smile and bid me farewell, presumably thinking that he wouldn't be seeing me again.

I walked down the road and straight into the first barber's shop I came to, returning to Minster about an hour later, clean shaven and sporting a very neat haircut, much to Trevor's obvious astonishment. As I had complied with his requirements, he felt obliged to take me on, all-be-it for a trial period. As I had never been to Kingston before and didn't know the area at all, it was decided that I should work in the control room where there was a large map of the area on the wall, taking calls and handing out jobs to the drivers - for at least a couple of weeks until I got to know my way around. A week later I was offered a room to rent in a house belonging to a young family in Hampton Wick, just across the river from Kingston – basically just somewhere to hang my clothes, sleep and wash.

Three weeks later I was wearing my smart, made-to-measure suit from Burtons and sitting behind the wheel of a new Volvo 144 automatic, heading off on my first mini-cabbing job. Most of the day-to-day work consisted of mini-cabbing, along with the occasional chauffeuring job carrying locally-based celebrities in and out of London. Mini-cabbing was charged by the mile, while chauffeuring was by the hour – and you wore a hat for chauffeuring. I was really settling into my new "career", working anything up to 16 hours a day and eating take-away meals on the job, so never really saw the young couple who were my landlords, except in passing and to pay them the rent once a week.

**

Having worked solidly through November and December, including Christmas, and then New Year, I'd been earning good money, but the long hours were taking their toll and I decided I needed a break - and maybe some female company. I consulted the little book in which I recorded contact details of the people I might want to meet up with again when back in the UK – and there was Christine in Brighton.

"Brilliant!" I thought - a weekend back in Brighton with old mates, including Gus if he was around, and enjoying a reunion with Chris - what could be better! I found a telephone box (remember, there were no mobiles back then), rang her number and waited. The phone was answered by Chris's flat-mate.

"Hi – could I speak to Chris please?"

"No, sorry – she doesn't live here anymore. She got a job in London and moved up there a few weeks ago".

Feeling suddenly deflated, with all my plans for a great weekend flying out the window, I was about to put the 'phone down, but then on the off-chance I asked, "Um - I don't suppose you have an address for her?"

"Yeah, hang on – here it is".

I took down the address, thanked her, went back to my Volvo, and took out the A to Z of London. When I looked up the address, I sat back in amazement, not believing what I was looking at. Out of the whole of Greater London, Chris's address was two minutes' walk round the corner from the room I was renting in Hampton Wick! I drove there, parked up and rang the doorbell. The door opened and there was Chris. She did a double take; the person standing in front of her was not the bearded, afro-haired hippy that she'd met in Greece, but a clean shaven, short haired person in a smart grey suit. She startled me by saying, "Oh, I was expecting you - come on in!"

What I didn't know at the time was that, a few days before she was due to leave for Greece, Chris and a friend had been walking along Brighton seafront; they were passing a fortune-teller at the entrance to the pier, when her friend suggested they should get their palms read. Chris wasn't keen, considering fortune-telling to be a load of rubbish, but was eventually persuaded that it would be a bit of fun. She had consequently been told that she was going on a journey overseas, but most of it would be by land. She would meet an Englishman who she was going to marry and, as soon as she saw him, she would know that he was the one – and they would have two children together. Although she had been quite impressed by the detail regarding her forthcoming journey, Chris had dismissed the rest of the reading as a load of baloney. But more of that later. I moved in with Chris the next day.

***

I continued chauffeuring and mini-cabbing through into May, when I got a despairing cry for help from Colin Payten. Frontier International had now managed to go bust two years running, but Colin wasn't going to throw in the towel that easily. He had virtually no funds available to him – certainly not enough to buy or lease vehicles, so he'd resurrected Frontier by selling trips and then sub-contracting to owner-drivers to actually run them.

One young lad in his early 20s had been on a Frontier trip to Russia and had had such a great time that, on his return, he had persuaded his father to buy him a Transit, before contacting Colin to offer his services as an overland driver. This was an offer that Colin duly accepted (the proverb "any port in a storm" comes to mind), and the first trip he gave him was to drive to Kathmandu with an empty bus to pick up eight passengers who were flying in from Australia for an adventure trip overland through Asia and Europe to the UK. Now the trip to Nepal was a tough challenge even for an experienced driver with the company and support of passengers, but to ask this "rookie" to take this on as his inaugural trip with no passengers on the outward journey was madness in the extreme. Consequently, two days before his clients were due to arrive in Kathmandu, Colin had received a telex message from his driver from Kabul, advising him that he'd had a mental and physical breakdown and that he wouldn't be going any further (it was still at least another seven or eight days hard driving from Kabul to Kathmandu.

Colin started 'phoning around in a panic; he needed an experienced driver who had done the India trip before, to fly out to Kathmandu and arrange transport to get them to the UK. I was getting itchy feet being 'grounded' in Hampton Wick, so two days later, with Chris's blessing, I flew to Delhi and then on to Kathmandu.

As I left our flat at 6am that morning to catch my flight, Chris was still fast asleep, so I left a note on my pillow, "I'll marry you when I get back. Love - Steve xxx".

A RESCUE MISSION

I walked into the Blue Star Hotel the following afternoon to find eight young people in shorts, sports socks and trainers sitting around the reception area, looking worried.

"Anyone here with Frontier International?" I asked.

"Ah yeah!" came the chorused reply.

"Well – my name's Steve and I'm your driver".

The was a group sigh of relief. "Great – we've been here three days now and we was all getting a bit worried, yer know".

"Sorry about that. Just one thing though – I don't have a vehicle for you at the moment".

"Ah, shit!"

What I hadn't taken into account, but very quickly realised, was that the world-wide oil crisis that had been caused by the oil embargo imposed on certain nations by OAPEC (later renamed OPEC) had caused oil prices to rise by nearly 300% by the end of March. This had badly affected many poorer countries, including Nepal, which relied on Indian companies for its oil supply. This had been exacerbated by a rail strike in India that month. Consequently, the overland companies that had been running trips from Europe to Kathmandu, including the Magic Bus ($70 US to ride the "hippy trail" from Istanbul to Kathmandu), were going no further than Delhi, as they couldn't be sure of completing the journey up to Kathmandu without getting stranded without fuel.

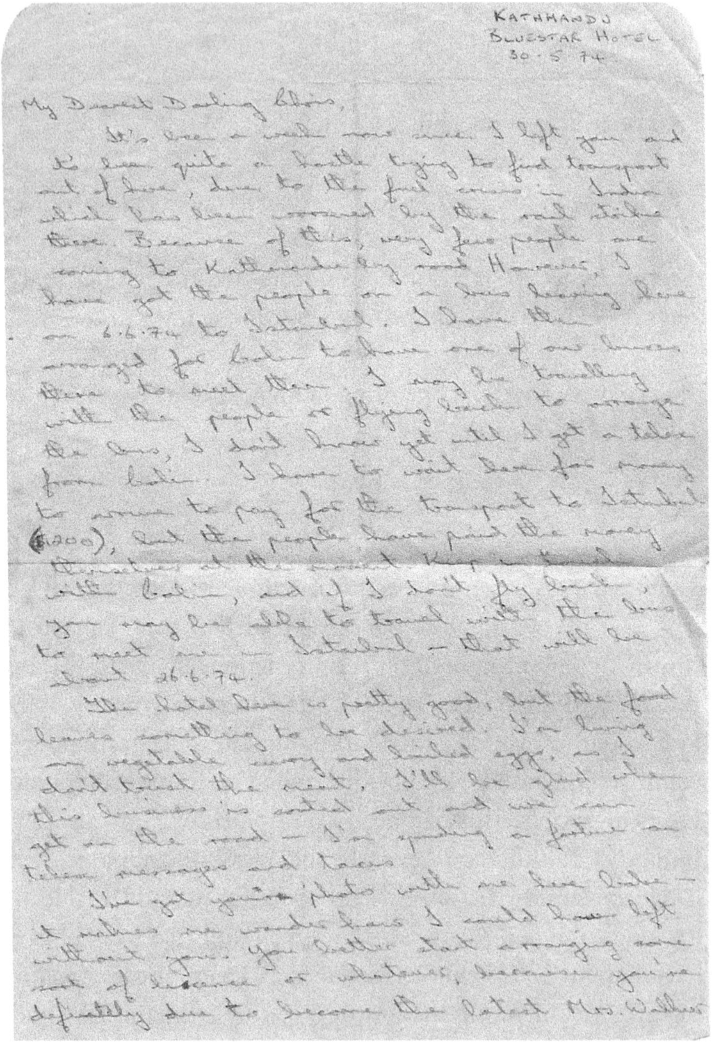

KATHMANDU
BLUESTAR HOTEL
30.5.74

My Dearest Darling Chris,

It's been a week now since I left you and it's been quite a battle trying to find transport out of here, due to the fuel crisis in India which has been worsened by the rail strike there. Because of this, very few people are coming to Kathmandu by road. However, I have got the people on a bus leaving here on 6.6.74 to Istanbul. I have then arranged for London to have one of our buses there to meet them. I may be travelling with the people or flying back to arrange the bus, I don't know yet until I get a telex from London. I have to wait here for money to arrive to pay for the transport to Istanbul (£1200), but the people have paid the money themselves at the moment. Keep in touch with London, and if I don't fly back, you may be able to travel with the bus to meet me in Istanbul – that will be about 26.6.74.

The hotel here is pretty good, but the food leaves something to be desired. I'm living on vegetable curry and boiled eggs, as I don't touch the meat. I'll be glad when this business is sorted out and we can get on the road – I'm spending a fortune on telex messages and taxis.

I've got your photo with me here [illegible] – it makes me wonder how I could have left without you. You better start arranging some sort of licence or whatever, because you're definitely due to become the latest Mrs. Walker

Letter to Chris from Khatmandu pt1

Letter to Chris from Khatmandu pt2

I sat down, ordered drinks all round, and spent the next 20 minutes explaining the situation and promising that I would be finding transport for them in the next few days so I could get them on their way. The group consisted of seven Australian nationals and a young Swedish woman who had been working for a shipping company in New Guinea. The Australians included Kevin "Kev" O'Connor and his girlfriend Robin. I learnt later that Kev had had a few run-ins with the local constabulary in Sydney over the years. Apparently, he had a propensity to "acquire" cars that he would then drive to another city to sell, before finding another acquisition to drive on to the next city to sell, and so on. The local police would occasionally enquire about Kev's whereabouts when cars had gone missing in the area.

"Not sure," Robin would respond when asked. "I think he's gone over the mountain!"

Ten days went by and, although I had all the hotel staff on a promise of £10 (a lot of money for them at the time), if they could find the required transport for me, I still didn't have it, and a number of the group becoming quite fractious. I was wondering how to resolve the problem when, lo and behold, a bus run by Swagman Tours, an Australian-owned outfit, rolled into town. The driver had been instructed to try and push through to Kathmandu, as they had a bus that had been garaged there for the winter the previous autumn.

A New Zealand lad had been sent on the trip as a co-driver, the journey down from the UK being his training trip. His job was to get the garaged bus checked over, serviced and ready to roll, before finding enough passengers to pay for the return trip Magic Bus style – straight through Asia and Europe without stops for sightseeing. Meeting up with him that evening, he was pleasantly surprised when I casually mentioned that I already had eight passengers lined up for him.

As the passengers would be missing out on the sightseeing element of the trip, I decided that I would fly back to the UK, acquire a minibus from Colin, drive down to Istanbul to rendezvous with them and then give them an extended tour of southern Turkey, Greece, the Dalmatian coast and Venice to help make up for what they'd missed out on in Asia. I agreed a price with Swagman, which my people would initially pay up front until I received money from Frontier. When I informed the group of the arrangement I'd made, they reluctantly agreed that I was making the best of a bad situation. I then telexed Colin requesting money to refund them.

A week later the bus was ready to leave, but I was still waiting for the refund money to arrive via American Express as they left. I calculated when my group should be arriving in Delhi and decided to wait in Kathmandu for the money and then fly to Delhi and rendezvous with them at the United Coffee House in Connaught Place in order to organise the money transfer. The money arrived later that same morning, three hours after they had left.

I waited four days before leaving Kathmandu, meeting with the group in Delhi as planned and heading off to the American Express office. It took most of the day to transfer my traveller's cheques to eight other people – Indians just love their bureaucracy! I bade a temporary farewell, promising that I would be waiting for them in Istanbul in ten days, when they were scheduled to arrive there, and headed for the BEA (British European Airways) office.

I approached the young lady at the bookings desk and asked if I could book a flight to London.

"Yes, certainly sir. Will you be paying in rupees, US dollars or pounds sterling?"

"Pounds, please".

"Thank you, sir. That will be £150".

This was a major problem – I only had £125 left. "Ahhh – do you have anything cheaper?"

"I don't think so – that is the normal price sir, but let me see". She studied the paperwork on her desk and then, after what seemed an eternity, said, "We have a cancellation on a flight this evening. If it is convenient for you sir, you can have that seat for £115". I handed the money over with a huge sigh of relief, took a tuk-tuk to the airport and sat with a cold beer, waiting for my flight to be called.

Arriving at Heathrow the following morning, I used my remaining £10 to travel down to Crawley, report back to Colin and collect a minibus for me to complete phase two of my rescue mission.

THE RESCUE

I knew Colin was short of funds, but it came as something of a shock the next day when I was presented, not with a Transit, but a Toyota HiAce – quite an odd, rather fragile-looking vehicle compared with a Transit! However, it was a case of being thankful for small mercies, so off I went to Hampton Wick and a reunion with Chris who, I was to discover, had just left her job, as it wasn't really what she had expected it to be. I recounted the problems I'd had in Kathmandu and explained the arrangements I'd made to rendezvous with my group and the trip I'd planned back through Europe.

Above Kavala on route for Istanbul, 1974

"So, fancy coming down to Istanbul with me? You could act as my courier".

"Yes!" was her immediate response. "I've already been making arrangements for us to move back down to Brighton, but we can do that when we get back!"

It was now late May; knowing that this was around the time of year when Roy Williams would be thinking of heading off to Greece for the summer, I thought I'd contact him and ask if he wanted a lift. "Absolutely!", came the immediate reply. So a couple of days later the three of us set off for Istanbul. We dropped Roy off in Kavala before driving into Turkey (a first for Chris) and on to Camping Londra to await the arrival of our group, who were due two days later.

The expected arrival day came and went with no sign of our people, so we waited and waited. Several days went by and the campsite fees were eating into my somewhat meagre trip funds. And then we had a slice of luck. We were befriended by a French trans-continental lorry drive, Jean-Paul, who was on his way back from Iraq, ("They are crazy there. You are driving along and then suddenly, goolie, goolie, wallop – someone is shooting at you!") He was stopping for a couple of days before heading back to Clapham, London where he was based. On learning about our situation, he and some of the other lorry drivers paid for us to join them for lunch and dinner at the local *meyhane* over the next couple of days and then those who were heading back home cleared out their food lockers and provided us with a variety of tinned foods – most of them without labels, so the only thing we could be certain of was the heart-shaped tins of ham. Apart from that, we weren't sure whether we'd be eating baked beans, tomato soup, beef casserole or sliced peaches!

***

We had been on the campsite for a few days when there was a flurry of activity, with the site facilities and grounds being cleaned and tidied. We were told they were getting ready for the visit of a gentleman by the name of Casper Humphreys, the operations manager of a large UK international travel company. He was coming to inspect the site and assess its' suitability for use by the company's coach trips. Chris's ears pricked up at the mention of the name. This was not a common name and she remembered an annoying, gawky-looking boy of that name from her teenage years back in Wales. The local girls' school in Bangor that she attended held a monthly dance when boys from the nearby naval cadets' college would be shipped in to partner the girls on the dance floor. This particular boy had become infatuated with Chris, making a beeline for her as soon as he arrived - and on one occasion, sending her a Valentine's card with a condom inside!

Mr Humphreys turned out to be a rather pompous individual, duly arriving the following day with his entourage in a luxury coach; Chris immediately recognised him as her ex-dance partner, although he obviously didn't recognise her. It was still early season and, as we were the only other Brits on the campsite and basically in the same business of tourism, he deigned to invite us to join him and his associates for dinner. Well, it was another free meal and so we sat that evening while he held court, patiently listening while he expounded on how he had bought his wife a little boutique business in Kensington to keep her busy while he was away. "But she still isn't happy!" he moaned. A little later Chris, who had been sitting next to him, decided to have a bit of fun and casually mentioned that she was blessed with the ability to read peoples' palms.

"Here Casper - let me have a look at your hand". He reluctantly acquiesced and as she took his hand in hers, Chris furrowed her brow in concentration and began to "reveal all".

"I can see water – yes, the ocean – and boats! I think you had something to do with the fishing industry, or - no, I think it may have been the navy - when you were younger. And I can see you dancing – with a girl that you had strong feelings for – a girl, let me see – quite tall, with fair hair. I think you may have been in love with her at the time. Her name began with the letter – G, was it? No it was a C – Carol - or maybe Claire? No – I think it was Christine!"

By this time our host was staring at Chris in disbelief and started to shake.

"Th-th-that's incredible," he stuttered, "How do you know all that?"

Chris looked at him and smiled sweetly. "That was me", she replied!

***

After ten days our passengers began to arrive at the campsite – not on their Swagman bus, but in dribs and drabs over the next couple of days. It transpired that their Swagman bus had begun to experience overheating problems a few days after leaving Kathmandu. The driver had been intent on pushing through to Europe and the UK and wouldn't stop anywhere to get the problem fixed. With the engine constantly overheating as they travelled through the Hindu Kush, the driver would stop by mountain streams, topping up the radiator with ice-cold water. Kev, (having a bit of past experience of motors) had pointed out that he should be waiting for the engine to cool down first, otherwise he was risking damage to the engine – but his advice had fallen on deaf ears. As they had continued through Afghanistan and Iran, basically without stopping other than to sleep in the bus for a few hours before moving on, their progress had become slower and slower until the bus finally expired in central Turkey. By this time some of the women were suffering from infections, as they hadn't been stopping anywhere to wash properly, and the passengers, in general, were on the verge of lynching the driver.

Kev had decided to head straight for the UK using local transport to take him to the nearest airport, while the rest of our group, including Robin, had used local buses and trains to complete the journey to Istanbul. Needless to say, by the time they eventually arrived at Camping Londra they were not in the best of spirits and were feeling somewhat aggrieved that Frontier had put them in this situation - some of them referring to me as "the enemy", although they were nonetheless mightily relieved to find me there, still waiting for them.

Due to their late arrival and the drain on my finances caused by the extended stay at Camping Londra, I decided that I would have to abandon the tour of southern Turkey so, after a couple of days in Istanbul for the group to enjoy a bit of sightseeing and recuperation, we headed into Greece. By the time we got to Athens, Sandy – one of the Australians, had developed a fever. On being admitted to hospital, she was diagnosed with hepatitis and consequently placed in an isolation ward.

After a few days relaxing in Tolo, we headed back to Athens to check on Sandy's situation. We were told that she would have to remain in isolation for at least another two weeks. I couldn't delay the trip any longer and, although it was a tough decision to make, we headed north, much to the annoyance of those in the group who felt that I was abandoning Sandy to fend for herself in a foreign country. We crossed into Yugoslavia, dropping down to the Dalmatian coast and travelling through to Venice before heading up through Austria, Germany and Belgium to catch the ferry at Zeebrugge.

As I drove off the ferry in Dover, I pulled up to Passport Control and Customs. The officer surveyed the minibus and asked where we were travelling from.

"I'm travelling back from Turkey and my passengers are travelling from Nepal".

His eyes lit up. "Can you pull over to the side there please".

Two officers then approached and asked us to unload everything from the roof rack and inside the minibus, before conducting quite an extensive search – presumably expecting to find drugs and/or other contraband, which, disappointingly for them, proved to be unsuccessful, other than an old flintlock musket that Sandy had acquired in Kabul as a souvenir.

"Who's the owner of this item?"

I explained that it belonged to a passenger that had been hospitalised in Greece and that Frontier would be holding it for her until she arrived in the UK.

"Sorry, but we're confiscating it. You're not allowed to bring firearms into the country without a permit".

"But it's an antique musket".

"Yes, but it still has a firing pin in place, therefore it's theoretically a serviceable weapon".

Leaving Sandy's musket to its fate, we re-loaded the roof rack and drove to London, dropping the group at Victoria bus station and saying our goodbyes, before making the short journey to Hampton Wick to collect our belongings, stay the night and then travel down to Crawley to return the HiAce and settle up with Colin. It had been quite a challenge and had proved to be a very difficult few weeks, but we had eventually got (nearly) everyone back,safe and sound from Kathmandu to London. It was time to head for Brighton.

We arrived un-announced at Gus's Brighton residence, a tiny one-bedroom flat above an empty corner shop, which he was renting it from Dave Latchford for £10 a week. We immediately commandeered the ancient sofa-bed in the lounge. Kev and Robin came to visit a week or so later. They had been re-united in London and stayed with us for a few days, sleeping in their sleeping bags on the lounge floor, before heading off on a European tour in an old VW Combi that Kev had acquired in London. Chris and a couple of friends took the corner shop and opened it as a local craftwork outlet, while I found bar work at a local pub and supplemented it with driving jobs for Dave's van hire business.

Chris and I were married six months later.

EPILOGUE

O verland gifted me some fantastic experiences, enabled me to visit some amazing places that I'd only dreamt of as a child and introduced me to some wonderful people – many of whom became life-long friends, remaining in touch over the years by telephone, letter, Facebook, and so on. From being a quiet, introverted, lad who was still living at home on an Essex council estate with his parents at the age of 23 and had no idea where his life was going, I became a confident, out-going adventurer, ready to take on whatever challenges life threw at me.

This is an update on some of the people and places mentioned in this book.

Gus Fraser, my mentor, eventually married my younger sister who presented him with three daughters. He ran his own successful fish restaurant in Brighton before they eventually divorced. Gus eventually went on to work with the UN and NGOs in Afghanistan, the RCA, Mozambique and various other war-torn countries in Africa. He now lives with his third wife, Meredith, in Australia. We are in touch on a regular basis. I shall be eternally grateful to Gus for providing me with the opportunity and inspiration to completely change myself and my life.

Having eventually failed to resurrect Frontier from its continuing money problems, **Colin Payten** moved his family to Australia where his career diversified from setting up an adventure holiday park in NSW, to running a mobile hog-roast BBQ service and captaining a trophy sports-fishing boat on the Gold Coast. Colin passed away on the 17th March 2023.

Micky Hynes set up his own private coach company following his marriage to Helen, an ex-passenger who gave birth to three strapping lads and became one of Chris's best friends, before the family emigrated around the mid-eighties to Australia, where they still live. We still correspond with Micky and Helen by Facebook, email and occasionally by phone.

Matt Davies lives with his wife Claudette in rural southern France. He has a business restoring old furniture and runs wine-tasting trips with his minibus to the chateaux in Bordeaux. He and Claudette have two lovely grown-up daughters. Matt and I are still in contact with each other and get together whenever the opportunity arises.

Stu Yates lived in France with his wife and two daughters for several years. He moved back to the UK a few years ago and now lives just a few miles from Brighton. I still see Stu about twice a year.

I heard very little from **Roy Williams** for a few years, only keeping in touch via his parents' address in Kent, until he turned up one Saturday afternoon in the early eighties at Gus's restaurant where I was helping out in the evenings as a waiter. He apparently went to the pub next door to wait for me to arrive for my evening shift, but failed to re-appear. I never heard from him again.

Mustapha Kasapoglu became an integral part of the overland scene in Turkey, providing a service for the majority of the overland groups that passed through Istanbul. Sadly, he was killed in a car accident in 1972 while returning from the Bulgarian border at Edirne. Istanbul was never the same place without him. He called all the drivers "abi", a Turkish word meaning "brother", but to most of the drivers he was a father figure and someone we could always turn to if we had a problem.

Towards the end of my time with Minster Cars, Chris and I had an invitation to the wedding of **Rabbit** and **Piglet** which was taking place just down the road from us. Unfortunately, I was attending a "London Courier" course for Minster that day, so was unable to be there. However, **Stu Healey** arrived in Dinsdale, a converted Bedford coach, dressed in top hat and tails like a knight in silver armour, to escort Chris to the wedding. Dinsdale was essentially a bed, bar and kitchenette on wheels with a huge built-in sound system, in which Stu had been living, parked up on Chiswick embankment. Stu helped Chris, dressed in a summer dress and a fashionable straw hat adorned with plastic fruit and flowers, up the steps to the front seat beside him. Placed on the engine cover between Chris and Stu was a bucket complete with a bottle of champagne. A couple of glasses were produced and filled and they proceeded on their way through Kingston. Dinsdale apparently proved to be quite a spectacle for the Saturday morning shoppers, with its elegantly dressed occupants sipping champagne and Wagner's "Ride of the Valkyries" blasting from the sound system!

Bettsie was a true Aussie, hard as nails and a good friend. I always said that had I ever got into trouble, he was the one person I would want standing beside me; he was the kind of person that would die for you. He eventually returned to Australia, married Norma, bought a plot of land on the side of a valley overlooking the Mitchell River outside a small town in Gippsland, Victoria and built his own house from wood that he'd cut out in the bush. Chris and I visited them in 2004. Norma told us how Bettsie had found a tall, straight ironbark tree in the Bush and, deciding it would make a great centre pillar to build the house around. He had cut it down and taken it to the local timber yard to be squared off, before digging a deep hole and setting the pole in concrete. It stayed like that for a while and they bought an old caravan to live in until the house was built. They'd invited friends round one day for a BBQ, when someone looked at the pole standing there and jokingly remarked, "I can see the house is coming along nicely, Bettsie"! To which Norma replied, "No worries, mate. We'll get round to it when we're ready – and when it's finished it'll all be paid for, while you'll still be paying off your fucking mortgage"

"That shut them up", she told us.

Norma presented Bettsie with a son, Steven, in '81 who eventually came to stay with us for a while a few years ago while working as a chef in Brighton, when he met his future wife, Collette. They all came back to Brighton a couple of years later for their wedding which took place on the bandstand on Brighton seafront.

Gary, to my mind, was one of life's victims. Although well educated, he had a naivety about him which got him into all sorts of strange situations. In 1974 he was persuaded by another ex-overland driver to go to Tanzania with him on the promise of work with a German logistics company organising the transport of heavy machinery from the coast to land-locked countries such as Zaire (now the Democratic Republic of the Congo), Malawi and Rawanda. The work didn't materialise and he found himself stranded in Tanzania, living with and being supported by a local woman he'd met. However, he was approached one day by an American who suggested that he might like to fly to Canada with him and join the organisation that he worked with – all expenses paid. Gary thought that it sounded a fair proposition under the circumstances, so he flew off to Canada with his new-found friend – and ended up working with Hare Krishna for the next few years.

He suddenly appeared out of the blue in Brighton a few years later and stayed with Chris and me for a few days. It transpired that the sect had paid for him to have a break back in the UK to visit his mother and friends. Having joined up with the sect, he had been required to shave his head, except for a top-knot at the back of the head, but had let his hair grow again on his return to the UK. However, when it did grow back, he found that he'd acquired a receding hairline, telling us that he had "gone bald while I was bald!" As he needed to support himself while he was in the country, he decided he would do what HK did to raise money in Canada. He bought an old van with some of the money he had, then found a Chinese wholesaler who stocked cheap hand-painted oil paintings from China (signed as "James Smith", or "Robert Jones", etc.) then drove to the wealthier suburbs around SE England selling them for whatever he thought people might be prepared to pay. In about three months he'd accumulated over £5,000, but he was worried that it might get him into trouble (alcohol was Gary's Achilles tendon), so he went to the HK temple in Watford and wrote them a cheque for £5,000.

He re-appeared a few years later; it transpired that he'd become disillusioned with HK, left the sect and joined up with someone he'd met who was hitch-hiking to Haiti where he intended to live a "hippy" life on the beach. Gary had been there for a year or so, sleeping rough and living out of trash bins. He stayed with us again for a few days, but he was in poor shape, suffering from malnutrition and arthritis. He couldn't drop his Haitian life-style – he would rise at around 5am and go off into Brighton to search through the bins, returning a few hours later with an "interesting" assortment of things that he'd found.

We lost touch with Gary and never saw or heard from him again.

As I said, **Kevin** and **Robin** (later to become Mrs O'Connor) came to visit us in Brighton before heading off on a European tour in an old VW Kombi that Kev had acquired in Earls Court. They re-appeared in December and stayed with us in our tiny flat, commandeering the floorspace in the lounge beside our sofa bed for their sleeping bags. I gave them a lift a few days later to Luton Airport for their flight back to Oz, in my uncle's old Transit van. We met up with them again 30 years later when we flew in to Sydney and just picked up where we had left off 30 years earlier.

Tolo became a second home to us and has remained so to this day. Chris and I have been adopted as family over the years by, among others, **Stavros and Vasilis** (our brothers), **Marika** (our little Greek sister) and **Vangelis** – Marika's cousin and now our nephew. Stavros sadly passed away on 5th April 2023; he will be greatly missed by all who knew him. **Vasilis**, his son **Vagelis** and daughter-in-law **Eleni**, together with baby **Kiki**, now live in Brighton and are part of our family.

As I finish writing this account of my overland years, Chris and I have been married for 48 years and have two wonderful sons, Dan and Nick, of whom we're very proud. The boys shared a house with Bettsie's son Stevie for about a year while he was in Brighton working as a chef a few years ago. Dan and his wife Izzie are now expecting their first baby, while Nick and his partner Saffron got engaged last Christmas and have just bought their first flat. Overland gave us the basis to build a wonderful life together, for which we will be eternally grateful.

.

www.ingramcontent.com/pod-product-compliance
Lightning Source LLC
LaVergne TN
LVHW051402080426
835508LV00022B/2936